"Immense capability and personal decency are the hallmarks of Charlie Baker's leadership style, and they're why he's the kind of governor other governors listen to. Both Democrat and Republican governors respect the results he's gotten, both in the public and private sectors. Any aspiring leader will learn about the power of purpose and possibility, along with how to pursue real improvements in peoples' lives, from this book."

—**DOUG DUCEY,** Governor of Arizona

"Governor Baker and Steve Kadish have written a road map to governing and 'getting stuff done.' Real-life examples of solving real-life problems. They're giving you a seat in the cockpit of government. A great read, with stories of true leadership and perseverance. Get this book!"

—**MICHAEL A. NUTTER,** former Mayor of Philadelphia; David N. Dinkins Professor of Professional Practice in Urban and Public Affairs, Columbia University School of International and Public Affairs

"In this book, Charlie Baker and Steve Kadish share their approach to delivering results that has enabled Massachusetts to make impressive progress on seemingly intractable problems and made Baker consistently among the most popular governors in the country. Their framework can be applied at any level of government, and I hope *Results* gets read by public-sector leaders and managers across the nation, including in Washington, DC."

—**JEFFREY LIEBMAN,** Malcolm Wiener Professor of Public Policy and Director, Taubman Center for State and Local Government, Harvard Kennedy School

"This book is a master class on making things work better and faster in government. The thinking, methodology, and case studies are delivered at a pace to inspire *and* be immediately useful. On behalf of my colleagues across government looking for a clear-eyed, practical approach—thank you for this gift."

—**JULIE LORENZ,** Secretary, Kansas Department of Transportation; Principal Investigator, Transportation Research Board on Innovation Cultures and Scenario Planning Practices

"What a tour de force! *Results* is a powerful distillation of what it takes to get things done. I love the examples that illustrate the framework's core elements and the integrative case studies that show the full framework in action. The practical lessons in each chapter provide a clear guide for anyone who wants to implement these ideas. Most of all, I found the book engaging and inspiring. At a time when people seem to have so little confidence that government can work, Governor Charlie Baker and his colleague Steve Kadish show how it can!"

—**NITIN NOHRIA,** former Dean, Harvard Business School

"With clear thinking and direct communication supported by facts and stories, Governor Charlie Baker and Steve Kadish show how government can bring about change and deliver results."

—**SYLVIA M. BURWELL,** President, American University; former Secretary, US Department of Health and Human Services

"This book is a practical and wise source for our time. It can help public servants everywhere to make progress in improving public services that really matter for its citizens."

—**ANNETTE DIXON,** Vice President, Human Resources, World Bank Group

"I loved this book. The Results Framework is not a theory but a practical, proven framework that can be used to develop innovative, data-driven solutions to solve a myriad of complex issues. All leaders and managers who want real, long-lasting results should learn how to apply the framework."

—**ANTONIA JIMÉNEZ,** Director, Department of Public Social
Services, Los Angeles County

"Two leaders who governed by 'grinding it out' explain how all public officials can do the same and why nothing less than our democracy depends on it. In *Results*, Charlie Baker and Steve Kadish deliver practical advice for public servants who want to set aside government-by-TV-appearance and the politics of vitriol and just get stuff done."

—**MITCHELL WEISS,** Richard L. Menschel Professor of Management
Practice, Harvard Business School; author, *We the Possibility*

"This book should be on the must-read list of all current and aspiring executives—in both the public and private sectors. For successful leaders like Governor Charlie Baker, solving problems is always about helping people. They know that getting the best results always comes down to the 'how'—and to putting the right team together in order to adapt when circumstances change and new information becomes available. *Results* highlights how important this type of thoughtful, common-sense problem-solving is and provides a playbook that leads to success. I highly recommend it."

—**PHIL SCOTT,** Governor of Vermont

Results

Results

Getting **Beyond Politics** to Get Important Work Done

HARVARD BUSINESS REVIEW PRESS

BOSTON, MASSACHUSETTS

Charlie Baker and Steve Kadish

The web addresses referenced in this book were live and correct at the time of the book's publication but may be subject to change.

Library of Congress Cataloging-in-Publication Data

Names: Baker, Charlie, 1956- author. | Kadish, Steve, author.
Title: Results : getting beyond politics to get important work done / Charlie Baker and Steve Kadish.
Description: Boston, Massachusetts : Harvard Business Review Press, 2022. | Includes index.
Identifiers: LCCN 2021058588 (print) | LCCN 2021058589 (ebook) | ISBN 9781647821807 (hardcover) | ISBN 9781647821814 (epub)
Subjects: LCSH: Industrial management—Handbooks, manuals, etc. | Success—Handbooks, manuals, etc. | Political leadership—Handbooks, manuals, etc. | Bureaucracy—Handbooks, manuals, etc.
Classification: LCC HD31.2 .B34 2022 (print) | LCC HD31.2 (ebook) | DDC 658—dc23 /eng/20211227
LC record available at https://lccn.loc.gov/2021058588
LC ebook record available at https://lccn.loc.gov/2021058589

ISBN: 978-1-64782-180-7
eISBN: 978-1-64782-181-4

To those who believe in public service,
in the good it must do, and who constantly
strive to deliver on its promise.

CONTENTS

PREFACE

In the summer of 2017, the two of us—Charlie Baker and Steve Kadish—started talking about whether we might put down on paper the practices we had developed over nearly three decades of working together—our organized methods for "fixing things." Our focus has been on the public sector—on pragmatic ways to get things done in government and in nonprofit organizations. We had experienced how government operates and believed that it could, and should, function better—not just for those who have special access, but for everyone. We had worked in both the private and the public sectors and knew that a simplistic fealty to "business principles" misses the mark. Public servants deserve a customized set of ideas, a framework, that pays attention to the peculiar dynamics of their work. If we got it right, we thought, we might even inspire folks in the private sector.

Upon my election as governor of Massachusetts in November 2014, I, Charlie, wanted to shape a different approach to governing, with the primary focus on delivering day-to-day services. I wanted to tackle our state's most significant problems through the prism of hard facts and real results, not by keeping a political scorecard. That was the approach we adopted right from the beginning of the Baker-Polito administration in 2015. The underlying philosophy would not be about winning—whether in marketplace competition or in political campaigns or in legislative sessions. It would be guided by a principle: the reason to do this hard work is that *democracy depends on it*. A core mission of government is to provide strong public services, and results are inherently rewarding: they fulfill the purpose of government itself, they make lives better, and they help restore our faith in democracy.

I spoke as directly as I could to this governing concept in my inaugural address in January of 2015, quoting one of the icons of Massachusetts politics, who happened to be a Democrat:

> Decades ago, John F. Kennedy stood where I stand today when he delivered a farewell address to the General Court of Massachusetts before traveling to Washington, DC, to become our thirty-fifth president. In that address, he said success in public service should be measured against four historic qualities: courage, judgment, integrity, and dedication.
>
> The president-elect defined these qualities for his time in office. Today, I offer them as this administration's compass in the years ahead—but redefined for our time.
>
> First, we must have courage to set partisanship aside and embrace the best ideas and solutions, no matter which side of the aisle they come from.
>
> Second, we must have judgment to make our government as efficient, responsive, and innovative as it can be.
>
> Third, we must have integrity to assure accountability and transparency, because when we make honest mistakes, they must be acknowledged and corrected.
>
> And finally, we must have dedication to serve the best interest of the public and only the public.

This book describes our approach and how we believe it can work at all levels of government across this nation. We came to the task with a shared respect for the American form of government of, by, and for the people, but also from different points on the ideological spectrum.

I, Charlie, grew up the son of a moderate Republican father (who worked in the Richard Nixon and Ronald Reagan administrations) and a liberal Democrat mother (a fierce advocate for education and services to support the most vulnerable in our community). Charlie Sr. was an assistant secretary of transportation under President Nixon and the undersecretary of health and human services under President Reagan. He staunchly believed in service and sacrifice. If my father gave me a vision of government service, my mother, Betty, gave me a simple practice. "You have two ears and one mouth for a reason," she was fond of saying. "If you're not listening, you're not learning."

Mom and Dad loved each other. They talked to each other. They respected each other. Our dinner-table discussions in Needham, Massachusetts, involved the issues of the day, and our parents expected my two brothers and me to participate. The model my parents set led me to never approach this work thinking that one side or the other is evil—or harbors bad intent.

I, Steve, am a native of Framingham, Massachusetts, and the oldest son of a businessman and a homemaker active in civic organizations. I grew up in a staunch Democratic household. After college and graduate school, I worked for various public interest groups and several political campaigns, including Ted Kennedy's 1980 presidential race. Those experiences pointed me away from a strict focus on politics and advocacy to what it takes to get things done. I found my calling behind the scenes, filling various leadership roles in and out of state government, primarily in health care, and at two universities.

We are a lifelong Republican and a lifelong Democrat. We are a Protestant and a Jew. Charlie is a politician, and Steve cannot speak on the stump. But we have a long history of working together in Massachusetts. In the William Weld administration, Charlie was twice a cabinet secretary and Steve had senior-level management and operations positions. When Charlie was CEO of Harvard Pilgrim Health Care, where our mandate was to right a sinking health insurer, Steve was senior VP for administration and project management.

We believe that good guys can win. That respect matters. That moderation is a way of coping with a complex world, and collaboration is not a dirty word. That an understanding of systems and management can be useful in making government function. And that government can be an engine of positive change, not just a hopeless bureaucracy.

As we started to collaborate on this book, we were struck by a column in the *New York Times* by David Brooks. "The truth is plural," Brooks wrote. "There is no one and correct answer to the big political questions. Instead, politics is usually a tension between two or more views, each of which possesses a piece of the truth."[1]

We wanted to capture that spirit—to underscore that the idea that one party, institution, or ideology has all the best answers is ludicrous and, worse, small-minded. We believe that to tackle the urgent issues of the day, we must understand the pain real people live through, vigorously seek facts, attack the reality of a problem, and refrain from personal political attacks.

Between other work and life events, we shared drafts, discussed structure, and debated the language of our ideas. By spring 2018, we had an outline of concepts, anecdotes, and case studies. In January 2020, we had conceived of a book in two parts and were discussing next steps.

When the Covid-19 pandemic struck, a few weeks later, it was pencils down. In August 2020, during the lull between the spring and winter case surges, we agonized over how, on the one hand, it was ridiculous to think about anything but Covid, and how, on the other, the book's lessons had only become more relevant. When a mob of violent rioters attacked the US Capitol on January 6, 2021, the very concept of our democracy and our government was threatened. Demonstrating that government *can* work became all the more vital. Later that spring, with a vaccination plan underway, case counts beginning to drop, and more kids returning to school, we returned to writing the book and including lessons learned from Covid.

This book comes from the two of us. With the exception of a few lines above and elsewhere, we speak as one. But please note: we do not use the royal "we" or the politician's "we." When we speak, it is in the first-person plural. If you see the first-person singular "I," you can assume that Charlie is speaking, unless Steve is identified as the speaker.

While this book is about the hard work of using the levers of government to achieve results, it is also a call to our better angels. A functioning government is a beautiful thing all by itself. But it is also fierce proof of our democracy. It can diffuse disillusionment and inspire confidence.

This work comes with a big piece of humble pie. We're always learning. Although our method can bring transformational results, it also involves course correction. We ask you to join us in remembering these words of Abraham Lincoln: "I shall do *less* whenever I believe what I am doing hurts the cause, and I shall do *more* whenever I believe that doing more shall help the cause." Lincoln was writing to Horace Greeley in 1862, and he continued: "I shall try to correct errors when shown to be errors; and I shall adopt new views so fast as they shall appear to be true views."

Our work embraces openness and accountability. In the words, again, of John F. Kennedy, "Let us not seek the Republican answer or the Democratic answer, but the right answer. Let us not seek to fix the blame for the past. Let us accept our own responsibility for the future."

With that, let us begin.

Reality

March 9, 2020.

I am on a plane, flying back to Boston early from a long-planned family vacation in Utah. While the rest of my family has been skiing, I've spent the past three days on the phone with my team in the governor's office and with public health experts. The crowds in Park City looked exactly as they have every time we've come here before: large, loud, and happy. Am I doing the right thing by flying home on my own and leaving my family to mix and mingle with the tens of thousands of folks from all over the place who are vacationing in Utah?

The state's first Covid-19 case presented in a college student who returned to Massachusetts from Wuhan, China, after spending the holidays with his family. His was the eighth reported case in the United States, and his condition was confirmed on February 1, 2020. He quarantined in his apartment, and that was that.

However, a few weeks later, dozens of Massachusetts residents came down with flu-like symptoms, and their physicians got in touch with our Department of Public Health. Their patients had all attended a conference hosted in downtown Boston by the biotech company Biogen. The gathering had brought together several hundred people from their offices in other states and a few other countries for a two-day meeting.

At this point in time nationally, test kits and approved testing sites were in extremely limited supply. The federal government was responsible for providing testing protocols, but, politely speaking, it botched the job. The Trump administration had known about the novel coronavirus since January and was promising the distribution, any minute, of the tests themselves and a speedy way to process them. Now days had turned to months. Without adequate and rapid-response testing, it was impossible to know what Covid's current status was or where the virus was going.

In early March, in what took just a few days, but what seemed like forever, the state's Department of Public Health prioritized testing the Biogen conference attendees from Massachusetts. The results were shocking. Of the then ninety-five confirmed cases in Massachusetts, seventy-seven were linked to that meeting. The Biogen gathering would become synonymous with the term "super-spreader event." Subsequent research estimated that as many as three-hundred-thousand Covid cases worldwide were tracked to this set of meetings.[1]

OK, I say to myself, so this thing is really contagious. How bad is this going to be? How long is this going to last? It is unsettling how fast this has all come on.

As I fly east, I'm pondering the numbers and what I'm going to have to do. Indisputably, the virus is in Massachusetts. Possibility has become reality. I'm going to have to declare a state of emergency.

It was the first of my "OMG" moments of the pandemic; I am sure a word with four letters formed in my mouth on that plane.

On March 10, I issued the emergency executive order. Such a declaration, in this case focused on the public health of our state, used one of the strongest powers I had as governor. Designed to enable swift action to prevent severe harm, this was a grave step that I and my predecessors have taken only a few times, with limited duration. At this time, none of us knew how long the emergency would last or how expansive that authority would become.

The next day, the World Health Organization declared the novel coronavirus a pandemic. There were now confirmed cases in 114 countries. The ease with which people continued to travel from country to country meant the virus was exploding across the globe. At that time, Massachusetts had only about 140 confirmed cases, more than half of which stemmed from the Biogen conference. We were very much a global destination, and people from all over the world were coming in and out of the state all the time.

A few days later, I announced the Covid-19 Response Command Center. It would be tied to every part of state and local government and would serve as our eyes and ears throughout the health-care community. If it turned out to be overkill after a month, we could always take it down.

I've always tried to operate on facts, first analyzing the problem and then focusing on what and how needs to be done to fix what's broken. For the previous few weeks, I had tried to learn all that I could about Covid and what others were doing to stall its transmission—and then act. However, those early days felt like steering an ocean liner filled with passengers, with few coordinates and no navigation equipment. The little information available—a mix of media reports, science articles, and anecdotal snippets—was a fog of data and hypotheses.

The stories from Europe, especially Italy, about the impact of the virus on hospital systems were unnerving. The basic health system was so overwhelmed with Covid patients that it was failing to attend to other critical health needs and emergencies. These stories were haunting.

In the end, what drove a series of decisions announced over the next handful of days was not what we knew but what we didn't know. Until our team had learned much, much more about this virus, we had to pause many aspects of daily life in Massachusetts to protect the public health and health-care system.

On March 15, I announced that Massachusetts would be one of the first states to close schools, bars, and restaurants (except for take-out or delivery), and I issued the most aggressive limit on public gatherings in the country. These emergency actions also ordered hospitals to postpone all elective surgeries, banned visitation at nursing homes and assisted living facilities, and required health insurance carriers to pay for telehealth visits.

About a week later, as the state's total Covid case count approached 650, I issued an emergency order for the continuation of essential services only and a stay-at-home advisory for everyone else. Allowing vital services only. Putting tens of thousands of jobs at stake. Threatening the very livelihood of families. The consequences of choosing to act immediately or take a wait-and-see approach would have far-reaching impacts. Inside the governor's office, we engaged in some heated exchanges. That made sense, as the consequences were so profound—unprecedented job loss versus safeguarding public health. But I understood that without assurance of the public's health, the economy could not thrive. I did not have all the information I would like to have had to make this decision, but time was the enemy. Each day, the coronavirus was proving increasingly ferocious, insidious, and lethal.

With this action, Massachusetts was one of the first states in the country to close all so-called nonessential businesses and issue a stay-at-home advisory. Those orders ultimately meant different things to different people in different states, but the overall message was the same: if you do not have to go out for something necessary, stay home. To this day, I consider that to be among the most drastic actions we took to stop the spread. And I'm well aware of the negative consequences.

We were all now at war with an enemy we could not see, but that threatened us all. Sometimes the governor's role is ceremonial, sometimes administrative, sometimes problem-solving. Sometimes, like this time, it is also visceral. I needed to summon everything I knew about leadership and call upon our collective courage. As I prepared for the announcement, I didn't know what was ahead. But I did know that this was a pivotal moment. At the press conference, after going through the details of which businesses and services would continue to operate, and assuring that grocery stores and pharmacies would remain open, I closed with these words:

> These are obviously profoundly difficult times. I have had numerous conversations with people who have lost their jobs and their businesses, and others that are struggling mightily to keep their doors open as best they can and pay their people. I also attended and spoke via livestream in two empty houses of worship, at Temple Emanuel and at Morningstar Baptist Church, over the weekend.
>
> As we drastically limit personal contact and force organizations and people to stop coming together, I also sense loss of purpose. Purpose is what drives us. Purpose is what fills our souls. Many feel lost, and I can see why. But here's the truth. We all have a role—we all have purpose— as we battle this disease. Protecting one another from the spread of Covid-19 by limiting physical and social contact and staying at home is profoundly purposeful. Every single act of distance has purpose.
>
> Our first responders and emergency and medical personnel—those who are essential to our success in battling this disease—need us all to do everything we can to reduce the spread. Reducing the spread, honoring these orders, honors and protects them—and you and your family.

There is purpose in these drastic changes in the way we live. We must all embrace this new way of life—and appreciate that here we can all find purpose as we battle this virus together.

Was this what all our work over the past five years had been in preparation for? Were the major problems the Baker-Polito administration had faced a kind of trial run for this moment: Transit system collapse. Massive budget deficits. Opioid epidemic. A multicommunity natural-gas-system failure. Were they all just a warm-up for everything that Covid-19 would bring?

With my announcement, we crossed the threshold into a new world. Covid-19 would be my focus and purpose for the next twenty-plus months. My method for "fixing things" was about to be put to the ultimate test.

Getting Important Work Done

In November 2014, I had been elected governor of the Commonwealth of Massachusetts, with Karyn Polito as lieutenant governor. I had lost my first race for governor in 2010, and the 2014 race was a nail-biter all the way. In the end, I collected only forty-thousand votes more than did my opponent, out of more than 2 million votes cast. There was no victory speech on election night. Only when I received a formal congratulatory call early the next morning did the reality of governing set in.

During the campaign, Karyn and I worked at a furious pace to meet as many people as we could. Karyn is from Worcester, in the central part of the state. She and her husband had two school-age kids. A lawyer and a businessperson, she had been general manager of her family's real estate development and leasing company with roots in the construction company founded by her great-grandfather, an immigrant from Sicily. The Polito name is well known in central Massachusetts—Karyn was a former legislator, and in 2010 she ran for state treasurer. Like me, she lost that year. Competent and engaging, she combines a warm smile with a direct professional demeanor. She is always prepared.

A campaign is about introducing yourself and explaining why you are running. If you get that far and still have people's attention, it is also about saying what you will do. Individual voters, local politicians, leaders of organizations, and the media are trying to size you up and see what you might do to address an issue that matters to them. You charge through hundreds of events, daily press releases, and phone calls before and after everything.

As a Republican in solidly Democratic Massachusetts, I had mostly small campaign events. Gatherings of a few dozen people took place after work in someone's living room or, as the workday was beginning, with some coffee in an office conference room. After my standard speech would come questions from the audience. If you're running for office, this is when you learn most of what's really on people's minds. After the formal questions and answers, some people would wait to talk to me—a kind of private word in an albeit awkward public setting.

In those moments, I was asked piercing questions about what I would do to fix things. I heard personal stories. Anecdotes about a state health program that could not tell you whether you had insurance coverage or not, even after you paid a health insurance bill. And quiet, painful accounts of opioid addiction. Moms and dads walked me through a litany of horrors associated with drugs that were literally stealing their children from them. Those stories stick.

In mid-December 2014 a few weeks after the election, Steve and I entered the Massachusetts statehouse. Although we had both spent considerable time in the building over many years, this was the first time we came as governor-elect and incoming chief of staff. We walked up to an elevator that would take us to the third floor and then into the governor's office. The next time I was to enter the building would be for my inauguration. I would be only the seventy-first governor since John Hancock, in 1780. As I crossed the threshold of the governor's office and walked past the portraits of my most recent predecessors, I thought about all the things that Karyn and I had committed to doing, all the people we'd met, all the stories we'd heard.

The question that was never asked on the campaign trail was now searing: *How?* How would we take an idea and make sure that it worked on the ground? How would we not only identify the problem but deliver on fixing it? I knew from experience that you can have money, people, and even goodwill and still not achieve your goal. How to get things done was too often the unsaid, underappreciated missing link.

On this day, Steve wanted me to visit the governor's office spaces to begin to literally visualize how we would work. Everyone assumed that I would take the big corner office overlooking Boston Common, as my predecessors had. Frankly, so did I—until I stood in the room. It was so damn formal. Historic paintings on the walls. Thick carpets. More museum than office. It was distant from Karyn, Steve, and the rest of the staff. We trucked down the hall. I picked out a room big enough for my desk, bookshelves, and a conference table. My lieutenant governor and chief of staff would be in the offices next door. It was a place where I could literally roll up my sleeves, quickly get to people, and spill my coffee. Pragmatic and straightforward, it marked the beginning of this intense focus on how. To ask how over and over defines the difference between rhetoric and results. It was time to move from the speeches of the campaign to the specifics of governing.

Right from the start, our mandate was to fix things. Asking Steve to be my chief of staff would signal that this wasn't politics as usual. Steve had held leadership positions as COO, CFO, and senior VP in both the public and the private sectors. He is an operations guy, a problem-solver—not a political operative. And that's what I was looking for.

It's not just that Steve is a Democrat and I'm a Republican that made my selection turn heads. The political cognoscenti expected the chief of staff to be the campaign manager or, at a minimum, a political consultant type. While I would continue to have political advisers, with the appointment of my chief of staff, I wanted to send a message that our administration would be focused on the internal workings of government to fix the problems I had been elected to address.

Later, the journal *CommonWealth* called Steve my "high-powered troubleshooter-in-chief." The article continued:

> Administration officials have even turned Kadish's name into a verb that describes the dissecting of a problem and the development of a roadmap to turn things around. "When an operation in government failed, Steve comes in and you're Kadished," says Jay Ash, Secretary of Housing and Economic Development. . . . Having Kadish parachute into your department is the "right combination of unsettling and motivating just the kind of creative tension Baker seems to be looking for," Ash says.[2]

In the years of working together, Steve and I had developed a methodology to move from identifying problems to achieving results—one that grew out of our experiences in government and was shaped by our experiences in the private sector. It was an approach born of necessity, because there were limited playbooks and less practical guidance for going from concept to delivery in the public sector.

In government, the high-profile focus is on policy, on legislative wins, and on budget dollars. We believe that as essential as budgeting and lawmaking are, they are only a piece of what makes government work. Our approach focuses on their necessary but sometimes over-looked companions: successful execution and implementation. We emphasize *results*, not political battles. Our approach maximizes the resources available and embraces the best ideas, no matter their source. It is an approach that bridges divides rather than exacerbates them.

I said in my second State of the Commonwealth address, in January 2017 that "wedge issues may be great for making headlines, but they do not move this Commonwealth forward." I added that "success is measured by what we accomplish together. Our obligation to the people we serve is too important to place politics and partisanship before progress and results."

For us, those words were much more than political platitudes. They were at the heart of our method. Now we have given it a name: the Results Framework. And we want to share it with those who, like us, want to change the way government works.

The Results Framework

The method we rely on is not revolutionary. It's evolutionary. It is a step-by-step process that leads to sustainable results. This replicable framework places a special emphasis on *how* to implement. It can be read, understood, and used immediately by those interested in improving the way government works in every state, county, city, and town. It's relevant for federal government. It's helpful to any public organization and to many private ones, too. At its core, the approach is about capacity and capability: about recognizing people's capacity to lead, evaluate, propose, and act; and about an organization's capability to focus, operate, and execute. It doesn't reduce important, complex issues to a single, simple intervention. Instead, it is a comprehensive approach that respects the complexity of implementing needed change.

Sustained change comes in incremental steps, each building on the previous one, providing a platform for the next. It does not come from the flick of a switch. Sustained change comes from grinding it out. Steady progress. Necessary course correction. Relentless advance leading to transformational change.

The Results Framework has four parts:

- People are policy (hire the leaders; build a team)

- Follow the facts (uncover points of pain; gather evidence)

- Focus on how (what to do; how to do it)

- Push for results (measure; evaluate; adjust; repeat)

People are policy > Follow the facts > Focus on how > Push for results

People are policy involves, first, prioritizing the selection of leaders and building the ability of teams so that together these *people* can conceive and actualize the policy, programs, and tasks to meet the challenge at hand. They are the drivers and doers; they provide leadership and ability. We emphasize people when we attack a problem to ensure that there is the capability and capacity to get the job done. We always begin with people, because while an existing team certainly possesses strengths, the leaders and staff may not have been able to address the problem. A new decree or policy pronouncement by itself simply will not work. This part of the framework calls for an overall reset to an initiative—to ensure hard-nosed evaluation of the facts, to develop the policy targeted to solve the problem, to aggressively implement the services called for, and to objectively measure the results.

Follow the facts requires gathering and evaluating data evidence and what we call *points of pain*. Facts define the problem and provide points of navigation for a response. To understand the problem to be solved, we solicit critical information, the data evidence, that describes the problem, and we listen for stories of the human points of pain that demonstrate real-world impact. The latter establishes concrete information that data alone cannot reveal. Points of pain brings the abstract down to the personal.

Focus on how develops a program for *what to do* and *how to do it*. "How" is the bridge between the problems that emerge from the data evidence and the points of pain and meaningful impact. This step ensures that proposed actions align with targeted results. This two-part step—what to do and how to do it—requires the greatest investment of attention, time, and resources.

Push for results uses *metrics* to determine actual performance and then make appropriate adjustments. Results are not an end point; they encompass objective evaluation. We make necessary adjustments—in the people involved, in our understanding of the facts, and in the what and how of the implementation—in order to push progress or address lack of performance. Once underway, the repetition of a particular cycle (measure, evaluate, adjust, repeat) leads to steady, sustainable results.

The Results Framework is a system of analysis, know-how, and persistence. No focus on any one part alone will succeed. For example, initially concentrating on developing a program solution (what to do) without following the facts may lead to an effort that doesn't address the need. Or having a good implementation plan (how to do it) but not the know-how and leadership from the right people (people are policy) can produce incomplete efforts and frustration. The emphasis on all four elements, with the essentiality of how, is what sets this approach apart from others.

Although we have experienced success with the Results Framework, we see it as a work in progress, a kind of continual beta testing for addressing huge, thorny issues in the public sector. We don't necessarily apply it universally. That said, on major change initiatives in which we have seen success—such as the state's overall response to Covid-19, the turnaround of a distressed child-welfare agency, the recovery of the public transit system, and the fix to a broken health insurance program—the principles of the Results Framework held up and helped us all.

When we missed something that shouldn't have been missed, or things slipped, or mistakes happened that should not have happened, we reverted to the principles of the framework as soon as we realized we needed to retool.

What Makes the Public Sector Different

Through the Results Framework, we acknowledge that the basic rules of engagement differ between the public and the private sectors.

Think about it. In the private sector, most decision-making is, well, private. Pros and cons are evaluated within the office walls. Any changes are effectively self-imposed. Unless the reason for the change is malfeasance, a massive failure, a meteoric rise, or a newsworthy one-off, the community at large doesn't hear about it and doesn't care. A report might appear in the business press, but for the most part the media stays away. When bad news tips into the public arena, it is typically short-lived. Spotlight on. Spotlight off.

In the public sector, policy and operational decisions play out in the open. Every decision, every service change, is fair game to be revisited, evaluated, and challenged by regular folks, interested parties, and aggressive reporters. That is as it should be. Decisions should have impacts. They involve trade-offs, priorities, and risks that can impact thousands, if not millions, of lives. Part of the decision-making, then, entails enlisting stakeholders, letting people know if they will be affected, anticipating what might go wrong, preparing a reaction, and anticipating adjustments. Successes will be taken for granted. Mistakes will be magnified. It's an ongoing public evaluation with an alert media ready to point out failures. Constant media requests. Constant critiques. Constant responses from pundits and commentators. Though it can feel as if every day is judgment day, that goes with the territory in the public sector.

The difference in the context for decision-making is just one thing that separates government from private industry. Let's break down some others:

- In the private sector, businesses make choices about what to do. It is inherently selective. In the public sector, the agenda is necessarily broad and often imposed from without. It can't be selective. Many things need to be attended to simultaneously.

- In the private sector, budgets can be flexible to meet needs as they arise. In the public sector, budgets are prescribed and literally take an act of the legislature to change.

- In the private sector, internal management determines who will do the work and how it will be performed. The CEO and leadership decide on partnerships, mergers, and whether to drop or add a product. The organization is free to pursue business best practices and encouraged to do so. In the public sector, the legislature can prescribe what the work is, how it will be done, and who may perform the services. It is a negotiated result that management, aka the administration, is required to implement, sometimes with consequential limits to the pursuit of best practices.

- In the private sector, success metrics are relatively simple and driven by bottom-line results. In the public sector, the meaning of success is continually debated and discussed.

- In the private sector, survival mandates continual innovation. In the public sector, change threatens the equilibrium of the status quo and the sway of powerful interest groups. Also, the ever-present risk of failure has public consequences.

- Most important, in the private sector, if an entity fails, ready competitors usually jockey to step in. In the public sector, although many services can be performed by other players, some functions that have critical consequences for individuals and communities can be performed only by government. Government services may be a last resort or a safety net, or a common good that benefits all. And it may be that no one else will provide them. Failure is not an option.

This concept of making government work, especially for those who depended upon these services with few other options, forms the rudder of my governing philosophy. Applying this rhetoric to people's reality means proactively working to meet the needs of historically underserved communities, removing barriers to access to services, and providing multiple ways to succeed to meet the demands of daily life and prospects for a better future. Thus, this was a critical lens for every major initiative—how to help those who needed it the most.

There is one more-fundamental difference, especially in the United States. At the core of our identity as a nation, our government is built on collaboration, cooperation, and compromise. Our founders believed in and structured our institutions to disperse power, authority, and decision-making.

Every step of public work is taken in concert and in constant engagement with steps taken by others. Every issue comes with myriad players, all with important perspectives, roles, and constituencies. Working with others is not just nice to do. It is necessary. No one gets their way. There is no single correct way to get things done. As a result, we need to rethink notions of opposition and to imagine new ways of working across divides.

The strength of the Results Framework is that it builds on a deep understanding of what makes the public sector different. It respects what otherwise might be considered "bugs" and makes them "features." The focus on people, facts, how, and results moves the discussion from social media stories and urban myths to objective information, evaluation, and action. In the end, we believe that our approach is not just about solving problems, but also about renewing faith in public services. Strong public services are an answer to public distrust and divisiveness. They can be a bulwark for our community values and our democracy.

How This Book Works

We have divided the book into two parts. In part 1 we detail each of the four steps of the Results Framework and how they function together. We use a variety of stories and examples, including some involving the Covid-19 response.

In part 2, we illustrate how the Results Framework operates in practice through four cases: health care, transportation, child welfare, and Covid-19. We tell these stories not because the work is finished but because we've made real progress in each case. Following the principles of the Results Framework led to meaningful impact that we believe would not otherwise have been achieved as quickly or as well.

The Results Framework provides a universal approach for improving the function of the public sector. So we include "Tips, Tools, and Tactics" boxes throughout that serve as step-by-step guides for applying these principles in any government or public organization (independent commission, nonprofit agency, health-care, or educational institution).

Who This Book Is For

We believe that government can and should work, and we want to help others who share that belief. We live in an era when stalemate, finger-pointing, and point-scoring seem to dominate Washington. The political dynamic is about differences—keeping political scorecards as if governing were a boxing match.

We like honest debate. But we like it better when problems are addressed.

We think of ourselves, and of anyone who follows our framework, as grinders. We try to work in the long arc of ideas, but we eschew the rhetoric of revolution, preferring to craft concepts that, if implemented well, can prove transformational. We look to see what's possible and push the edge. And if we don't get it right, or as good as it might be, we make adjustments as quickly as we can. Although this work has a dollars-and-cents aspect, it's fundamentally about human impact—about solving problems for people.

We are not trying to bend government to the ways of the board-room or the C-suite. We can learn lessons from the private sector—and we do. However, real differences in the rules of the game make how to get things done in the public sector its own subject. We embrace those differences. They are essential to the give-and-take of our democracy and what it means to govern. We don't care if you're a Democrat, a Republican, an Independent, or a Green. We care about when things don't work and what to do about it—the nuts and bolts of delivering public services.

In the public sector, we're not about fail fast, risk and reward, or unbridled entrepreneurship. But problem-solving requires taking a risk to create change, because continuing to do what was done before created the problems we now face.

So we encourage public-sector problem-solvers to take some risks, to challenge the obstinance and kryptonite-like power of the status quo, especially in large bureaucracies. Don't be afraid to take risks just because doing so is hard, different, or new to the organization. Learn from mistakes *and from successes*. Be prepared. Do your fact homework. Put together the people and resources. Crystallize the problem to solve. Be concrete about goals and relentless about imple-mentation. Measure the results, evaluate, and then adjust. You will make mistakes. And you can learn from them, recover, make pro-gress, and then succeed.

The examples we use come from our home state, but the lessons of the Results Framework are not limited to Massachusetts. Govern-ments everywhere and at all levels are grappling with similar issues—in health care, transportation, child welfare, telecommunications—and with similar bureaucracies and barriers to change. US Supreme Court Justice Louis Brandeis described states as "the laboratories for democ-racy" so that the experiences of one state could be translated to other states and nationally. We view the specific stories from our state as fulfilling this idea.

We know it's harder to take a step forward than to stay in the pack. As Teddy Roosevelt said, "It's hard to fail, but it is worse never to have tried to succeed."

We hope you will lean in, go forward, and tackle the gnarly stuff. The Results Framework and the stories that follow will give you the tools, a push, and even some added confidence.

The need is urgent. We can and must do more and do better. We hope this book will help launch new public initiatives and offer a practical way to reset existing efforts that may be struggling. We welcome your ideas for new models and methods. As the issues only get more complex, and the need to resolve them more urgent, we need all our best thinking and efforts.

The terrain is fraught; the problems numerous and complex. And it may seem that no good deed goes unpunished. But the opportunity to help is real, and the call to public service is human, decent, and noble.

. . .

As I left the press room on March 23, 2020, after imposing a dramatic set of actions to protect our core public health, I wasn't sure what the future would bring for Massachusetts, for the United States, or for the world. We were grappling with what the pandemic and our response to it would mean for our lives and the people we love. But I was sure about one thing: I would rely on the principles of the Results Framework. (See Chapter 8, which is devoted to the Massachusetts Covid response.)

We had launched this approach when I was elected in November 2014. People is where we always start, and so we did as I was building out my cabinet, a story we turn to in the first chapter.

PART ONE

The Results Framework

Four Essential Steps to Getting Important Work Done

1

People Are Policy

The spotlight on the appointment by newly elected mayors, governors, and presidents of cabinet secretaries and other leaders has no analogue in the private sector. The election happens, and almost immediately attention and speculation shift to people and positions. The media and the political cognoscenti examine every name and pose suggestions of their own. All this is for good reason: These choices say much about what qualities the person making the appointments values. They are signals for how an election will translate into governing.

In the fall of 2014, finding a secretary of transportation was proving to be a more difficult task than I thought it would be. Yes, it was a monster of a job—roads and bridges, trains and buses, highways and skyways. The work touched every community and everyone with a driver's license or a desire to get somewhere. Many of the state's largest capital projects were managed here, as well as the day-to-day maintenance of hundreds of miles of roads, vehicles, and tracks.

Transportation was at the center of how everyone and everything moved from place to place—and that was the point. I was looking for someone who understood that transportation was a means, not an end. Too many people in transportation think the name of the game is accomplishing one-off projects, whether widening a road, repairing a bridge, or adding a transit stop. I thought of it as access— to jobs, school, and medical care, as well as to the daily stuff of life, from food shopping to meeting friends. I also knew that transportation was at the nexus of housing, the economy, and the environment and that we were way behind where we needed to be.

While I had liked the candidates I had been interviewing, I knew the importance of getting outside your circle, beyond the usual suspects. I was looking for what I called a "50 percent player"—someone who thought we had real issues and wasn't interested in making things just 5 percent better, but dramatically better. I called a friend who had spent much of his career in public transportation and asked him for suggestions. He had one name for me: "Stephanie Pollack."

Hmmm. I knew who she was. She had sued the Weld administration on several occasions some twenty-five years before, when she was a senior attorney at the Conservation Law Foundation, and I was secretary of administration and finance. She was currently at Northeastern University. She was a strong transit advocate and a well-known, well-respected, liberal Democrat. I expressed concerns about our potential differences, and my friend said, "Call her. You two will like each other."

I did call her, which surprised her, and asked her to come by to talk about transportation. Later, we both admitted to one another that we expected the meeting would last about ten minutes. Instead, it lasted two hours. The longer we talked, the more I thought she was the right person for the job. She was sharp, creative, unafraid of the challenges, and very, very informed. About an hour in, I thought to myself, "This is the one."

As she got up to leave, I said, "I'd like you to come back and talk with Karyn Polito and Steve Kadish, but I gotta say right up front, if I hire you, my friends are going to kill me." She looked up at me and snapped back, with a smile on her face, "And if I accept the job, my friends may *never* again speak to me." Well then, I thought, maybe we would have more time to get the work done. On some level, I was surprised at how aligned we were on what was broken and what needed to be fixed. And while I knew choosing her would cause some surprise, I was sure she would not be afraid to take on the mountain of work that needed to be done. She would be the first woman to run the Transportation Secretariat, and I made clear to her that on that issue, I would have her back.

Looking back nearly seven years later, Pollack and her team played a pivotal role in the rescue and investment in our public transit system, found innovative ways to proceed with long-stalled projects, and developed important programs to support transit-oriented jobs and housing, pedestrian- and bike-friendly streets and downtowns, as well as policies to curb transportation-related carbon emissions that led the nation in new thinking. In the spring of 2021, Stephanie was appointed to a senior position on the Biden administration's transportation team.

People Are Policy

The concept of people are policy provides the structural umbrella for the Results Framework. The best ideas are only abstractions until people act upon them. While we may be in the midst of learning about the problems, when we mean to act, we always start with *people.* For a couple of decades now, I have been saying "people are policy." This phrase captures for me an essential idea regarding just how important prioritizing people can be, especially in the public sector. Typically, policy is considered the first order in government. It's discussion about policy that brings out possibilities, passion—and partisanship. Policy, whether on climate change, voting rights, or anything else, can and does dramatically affect our lives and communities. Furthermore, the media focuses its attention on policy fights—in the legislature, in the administration, or in the courts. The front page is often a running policy scorecard.

Unfortunately, when it comes to policy, the gap between intentions and implementation can yawn wide. Policy is important in its own right, but by itself it is simply not sufficient. Effective policy can only be achieved when there is effective implementation and operations. Effective operations needs policy to provide guidance and direction, but it needs people to get the work done.

The phrase "people are policy" underscores the interdependency of policy and operations. By making it the overarching principle, we put the emphasis where it belongs—on the individuals and teams who define policy and, just as important, drive change and deliver results.

People are policy means selecting women and men who understand the task at hand and what is needed to successfully deliver measurable, on-the-ground results. The capability, experience, and values of the people empowered through each step of the Results Framework allow us to realize the implementation of policy—and ensures an initiative's success. Steve and I start here because you need to get this right or all else founders. This so-called soft stuff is in fact the hard stuff of governing.

Selecting a cabinet while the public watches

Right after the November election in 2014, while we were building the team in the governor's office, I needed to appoint eight cabinet secretaries to oversee some 150 state agencies. Each agency had its own commissioners, program directors, and budget, legal, and other leadership positions. Time was precious. Each hour, each day mattered. How soon would the cabinet be complete? How many other key positions could be filled before my inauguration and in the weeks to follow? Every appointment means vetting potential candidates, conducting interviews, and completing background checks.

In the private sector, even at nationally recognized firms, when a new CEO is named, a quiet period follows. The CEO is given time to evaluate personnel with limited, if any, media attention. The CEO does not pick the management team with a public shot clock running.

After I was elected, I had set aside time each day to review candidates for the cabinet and a few other key positions with Lieutenant Governor Polito and Steve. The transition team had prepared org charts and other general information that provided useful structure. In these meetings, I would describe what I was looking for in a particular role—the kind of experience and the skill set I thought would be required to succeed. I knew that although the governor's office is the hub for so much from day to day, only a fraction of what happens in state government is seen or affected here. It is the cabinet and agency leaders who make things happen.

It wasn't only outside expectations that drove us; we were aware that the faster we built the team, the faster we could focus on the work at hand.

I filled a few spots immediately. For the others, we quickly established a pattern whereby one of us would have a preliminary discussion with the candidate and then, if appropriate, set up two follow-up interviews. Even if I knew the candidate, I wanted to do an interview for the role. Knowing someone and considering that person for a specific position are not the same.

We wanted certain qualities in all candidates—smart with solid experience, a strong work ethic, public-spiritedness. And *no jerks allowed.* Strong personalities, commanding presence, and smart as hell—check a big YES on all three. But no loudmouths, know-it-alls, and over-the-top arrogance. We were going to be working *with* one another. A lot. Early morning, late at night, weekends. In the interviews, we each brought different questions. I was evaluating subject-matter knowledge and the ability to articulate problems and potential solutions. Karyn focused on candidates' understanding of legislative and other key relationships statewide. Steve scrutinized their approach to running organizations and getting things done. Together, we tried to assess capabilities, comfort with complexity, the ability to problem-solve, and core values. It was an intense evaluation of know-how, as in knowing how to match facts and programs, knowing how to work with others, and knowing how to get things done.

By January 21, the cabinet was in place. My first three picks were a Democrat, a Republican, and an Independent—in that order. The complete team consisted of four Republicans, three Democrats, and one Independent, and it included a mix of five men and three women as well as one person of color. But it was know-how, diversity of experience, and decency that I was looking for. Their first task: to build their teams.

Those cabinet appointments made it clear from the outset that my administration would be bipartisan. In appointing Steve, a Democrat, as chief of staff, I formed the only Republican governor/Democratic chief of staff team in the nation. Like the cabinet, the staff of the governor's office was composed of Republicans, Democrats, and Independents.

But there was more to it. For me, the people I selected to be on my cabinet and to serve in some of the most important positions in state government did not reflect merely a concern about ensuring broad party affiliation. It flowed from a desire to make the work not about title or appointment, but about public service.

Speed Matters.
So Does Quality

Tips Tools and Tactics

When we have made the people decisions our top priority from the outset—defining the skills and experience needed, clarifying roles and responsibilities, and actually building the team— we have had the most and the fastest success. The times when we failed to make this a priority, we have seen slow starts and ineffective progress—to be resolved only by then going back to address the people issues.

It is possible—and necessary—to move both quickly and carefully to gather your people. This is not something to squeeze in, especially at the beginning of an initiative. *This is the work.* Dedicate the time.

Follow these steps:

1. Set an overall target date to have the team in place.

2. Identify the critical competencies and characteristics needed.

3. Outline the positions and responsibilities in an initial org chart.

4. Build your best team. Not only dive deep into your networks for people you know can do the job, but be intentional about building a diverse pool of candidates. Make a list of internal and external candidates for each role.

5. Ensure that all involved prioritize completing the interviews.

6. Check for the "collaborative gene." Working in the public sector is not "my way or the highway"; it's a team sport.

(continued)

7. Include people who know basic public-sector rules and culture, including collective bargaining. This avoids mistakes and speeds things along. A bureaucracy doesn't have to be bureaucratic, so it helps to have team members who are familiar with basic operations.

8. Select the best people; talent attracts talent. Consider tapping the incumbent. Promote top performers. Recruit from outside. Insist on diversity. Seek a combination of new and current people.

9. Update and share the org charts.

10. Gather the team and rock and roll.

Reflecting back now many years, these qualities have been the standard for me and my team. And they provide a compass for the Results Framework.

Hire the Leaders

My father used to say that people get fired by their bosses long after they get fired by their peers and their subordinates. Our advice to any new executive or manager charged with addressing a major issue is to first select the people who will lead the team and the others who will have critical roles in the effort.

Always remember that great teams do great things. Mediocre ones, not so much. In the public sector, especially at the start of a new administration, it is easy to get distracted and tangled up in the day-to-day. It takes focus and diligence to build a great team. Time must be spent making calls, reviewing candidates, shaking the trees. In fact, in our experience, the bigger the problem, the greater the change in people will be required to develop, appreciate, and pursue the work that needs to be done. So prioritize the time you need early on to build the team and create the necessary capacity—first.

This work should be done in days or at most a few weeks. As you take on your new role, whether it is for a specific initiative or to run an agency or a program, everything else can seem more important. You will have a press of people to meet, immediate decisions to make, and urgent matters to address. These and other obligations will quickly fill and overwhelm your calendar. Before you know it, not only have a few days gone by, but days have become weeks, and weeks have become months. Yes, some immediate brush fires have been put out. But your organization's capacity, and its ability to address its challenges, will be driven by the quality of the team you build.

While there is no simple checklist for selecting leaders and team members, there are baseline requirements: know-how, collaborative spirit, and diverse backgrounds.

Knowledge and know-how

I have always been biased in favor of people who know their subject matter. This is not only about how much they know, or how smart they are, or how knowledgeable they may be on the issue. Knowledge is always important, but by itself, it is not enough. This is about how the facts and ideas come together into context and policy, and eventually into strategy and operations. I care about the idea, and I care about translating it into reality. This is about a person's knowledge and ability to know how to get things done. As a CEO, a cabinet secretary, and a governor, I have learned that this balance of abilities points to the best person for the job.

However, the combination of knowledge and know-how in one person may not always be possible. In fact, it is a rare combination. The brilliance of creating an idea, policy, and even an undergirding philosophy to impact a problem may be different from the brilliance of making the ideas a reality. But it is possible to build a leadership team with both of these qualities by finding them in separate people. Sometimes we had a strong policy person as the overall lead and then we hired people with operations experience to be a complementary part of the team. We have also had the opposite situation: a strong ops person at the top, with others on the team skilled at thinking not "how to do it," but "what to do."

The collaborative gene

I want leaders who realize that this work is a collective effort, process is important, and results for customers is key. I look for people who acknowledge that while the CEO has a critical role, it takes a team to succeed. I need to see that candidates for leadership positions don't just understand but believe in the various roles of those involved in governing. "My way or the highway" just doesn't work in the public sector. There's far more finding of common ground in public life than many people appreciate. Part of the way you get things done is by recognizing that there's more than one way to think about an issue and more than one way to deal with it. Getting things done in the public sector is grounded in collaboration, cooperation, and compromise.

While we had good success in recruiting and promoting talent, we are super-aware that "the book doesn't always match the cover" and that the need to make staffing adjustments was just as important as the need to make policy and operational ones. We made a mistake at one high-profile agency where, in selecting the leader, we focused on the person's technical and management experience, without digging into how the person worked with others. While this person made some notable accomplishments, overall the agency lost ground—and lost confidence. As soon as we realized this, we changed the leadership. Although we can't cite its specific origins, this oft-quoted, possibly African, proverb says it all: "If you want to go fast, go alone. If you want to go far, go together."

Diverse experience

Immediately after my election, we began to discuss how the governor's office itself would work. We knew that its basic functions included legislative affairs, constituent services, general counsel, policy, communications, and scheduling. We wanted to add two new functions: the Office of Access and Opportunity, and the Strategic Operations Team (more on this later). To be clear about their importance, we would have each report directly to Steve. The Office of Access and Opportunity's purpose was to be the administration's lead for increasing the diversity of our employees and of the firms doing business with the state. We knew that to do the best for the Commonwealth, we needed to proactively involve all communities as part of the work—directly, as managers and staffers, and as state contractors. We wanted this strong example and message to come right from the top.

The Access and Opportunity team made recommendations for filling boards and commissions; worked closely with the state purchasing agency to increase the number of minority- and women-owned businesses performing work on state contracts, including LGBTQ; and expanded recruitment efforts. At cabinet meetings, we had periodic reviews of management and staff diversity along with updates on the diversity of our state spending. This team also worked to reestablish the Black Advisory Commission and Hispanic Advisory Commission, and worked closely with Asian Advisory Commission, to solicit recommendations on how best to support their communities.

While we as an administration made steady progress over our first five years, the murder of George Floyd by Minneapolis police officer Derek Chauvin and the hate-crime shooting of eight Asian women in Atlanta—among many other events—showed us how much more was needed to address the fundamental structural inequalities in our society that were based on race. Addressing these inequalities had to be part of our hiring and appointments.

During 2020, as governor, I had a unique opportunity to make not one but three nominations to the Massachusetts Supreme Judicial Court. These were among the most important people decisions I would make. I pushed for diversity in the candidates that I would be interviewing, knowing that people with great legal skill, knowledge, and experience are present in all of our communities.

I was thrilled when Justice Kimberly Budd, whom I had previously appointed to the SJC, agreed to be nominated to serve as Chief Justice. She was an outstanding jurist and leader in the court system. She would be the first black female to the lead the court. Next, I nominated Dalila Argaez Wendlandt, whom I had previously appointed to the Appeals Court, to be the court's first Latina justice. Trained as an engineer and as an attorney, Justice Wendlandt brought a broad range of wisdom and experience. My final nominee was Boston Municipal Court Judge Serge Georges. The son of Haitian immigrants, Justice Georges had been raised in the Boston neighborhood of Dorchester and would be one of only a handful of district court judges to ever be elevated to serve on the state's highest court. A former litigator, Judge Georges had represented clients in criminal and civil matters and would bring a distinct voice and real-world experience to this highest court.

The Governor's Council approved all three nominees. Never in its more than three-hundred-year existence had the highest court in Massachusetts had three sitting judges of color. Going forward, the Supreme Judicial Court would be one of the most diverse top state courts in the nation.

Rhetoric meets reality. Our diverse society gives us a plethora of capable and compassionate professionals. Here and throughout our work, I wanted to take full advantage of the strength and diversity of our citizens.

Build the Team

People are policy means much more than just picking the leaders. People are policy is about the total organization's capacity to perform. It means keeping an eye on how to build a *full* team. In many organizations, and especially in the public sector, we don't pay enough attention to having enough people with the skills and experience to tackle a problem. More work is just piled upon existing staff and managers. This aspect of people are policy—creating capacity—entails extending permission to engage more staff, seek out consultants, or find colleagues in other offices or agencies who have specific skills for specific tasks.

Sometimes, specific expertise in short bursts (hours or days at a time) does the trick. But typically we need full-on additional support—more full-time employees for weeks and months. Giving your organization the people to perform successfully might just mean that more bodies on a task will get it done faster. It might mean that new individuals can add new skills not yet in the organization or can enable you to build what is needed—by improving IT systems, writing guidelines, crafting a performance report, or digging into project management. It might mean shifting current staff to this new assignment (and backfilling the position as necessary). Building the team is synonymous with building the necessary people capacity.

New people and veterans

We've usually done better at addressing major issues when we relied on a mix of new people *and* some incumbents in leadership positions. Every organization has strong managers and staffers who should be identified and appropriately recognized. But it is not enough to make org chart changes with existing personnel. We have found that in organizations facing problems, although the staff and managers may be able to identify what's not working, and in some cases may know what needs to be done, in the end, no or limited action has been taken. Why? In some instances, they lack the know-how to do things differently and the perception to see what's needed. And sometimes, current staffers know what to do but don't have permission to act. In short, improvements weren't made until new people created a path forward.

New people bring a fresh combination of knowledge, experience, and approaches. Together with known players, they create a healthy and productive dynamic that respects both experience and innovation. Ideas for improvement, options for implementation, and the rollout of changes are all better as a result of this constructive tension.

Hail to the chief operating officer!

In the public sector, maximum attention is too often given to budget and policy and not enough on the delivery of services. We see this reflected right at the top of many agencies. Take a look at the org chart. In the public sector, key roles surrounding the CEO typically include chief of staff, chief financial officer, general counsel, communications director, policy director, and leads for specific programs. All important, to be sure. But where is the single person dedicated to orchestrating all that is necessary to support the delivery of services? In the private sector, in any organization of size, that's the chief operating officer. Prioritizing and not overlooking this leadership position is a lesson we take from the private sector for how to get things done in the public sector.

The COO is the person charged with making the engine run. That broad management responsibility is focused on the excruciatingly detailed work of logistics, technology, people, and facilities all coming together to deliver a product or a service. It may include budget and finance. The COO works closely with the chief of staff, the person in charge of policy, and other agency leaders.

While in the public sector, the role may have a different title (i.e., assistant commissioner, undersecretary), the chief operating officer position is best filled by someone who has had previous operating and management experience. Whatever it may be called, if there is not a position fully dedicated to this work, then create it.

A change catalyst

There's a physics to how a public agency operates. It may not always seem so to the people it serves, but a public agency is always running at what it believes is full capacity. The best agencies can simultaneously provide services and handle some improvements. But if an agency is in crisis, it needs a different kind of help. It simply doesn't have the capacity to make the changes necessary. The status quo got things to where they are, and it will continue without significant intervention. To fix things, disruption is required. Support must come from outside the agency.

A dedicated, mission-oriented team can serve as a catalyst for change. This team's leader and members, consisting of new and current staffers (and consultant support as appropriate), must have knowledge, experience, and expertise to move beyond the status quo. In the military, the dedicated team equates to missions. In management consulting, the dedicated team equates to the client project.

In *The Other Side of Innovation*, Vijay Govindarajan and Chris Trimble lay out the idea of a "performance engine" and an outside dedicated team. The day-to-day running of the agency is the performance engine. They write: "It is a mistake to ask the Performance Engine to operate outside the confines of its specialty. The limits are rigid. Simply asking everyone involved to think differently or behave differently will not work. If you ask the Performance Engine to tackle a task that is outside its limits, it will either fail at the task or succeed only by disrupting existing operations. Neither outcome is acceptable. Building a dedicated team is preferable."[1]

Let's be clear about what we mean by "dedicated." At the beginning of one of the Covid-19 response initiatives, Steve was describing the need for a team dedicated to the project. In response, one project leader said that they were all "dedicated" to making this work. It occurred to Steve to ask how much time they were each spending on the project. The answer was 10 percent to 20 percent. That's not what we mean by dedicated, no matter how fine the intentions. We mean 100+ percent time devoted to the effort.

And let's be clear about what we mean by "mission-oriented." It's not about describing the organizational mission, which has a limitless time horizon. Mission-oriented means deliberately limited to the resolution of a specific problem in a specific amount of time. It defines the problem, evaluates the facts and programmatic options, and focuses intensely on how to get the job done.

Dedicating people fully to a single effort is actually hard to do, especially in the public sector, with its tight budgets and often rigid approaches to doing the work. It involves taking some of your best people off their current work and bringing in some new people, not just for a weekend or a week but for the weeks and months it takes to design, develop, and implement the changes needed. It requires a shift in resources to align with the change in priorities.

An opportunity to provide true value-added support

In the governor's office, much of the staff must deal with topics immediately at hand and then move on. The sheer number of concerns and the constant media attention demand rapid cycle times for response. However, many of the most serious problems didn't develop overnight and can't be resolved in a day. We wanted to offer our agencies real value-added support. We knew from experience how important it would be not only to have the intent, but also to resource the change effort.

We created the Strategic Operations Team, a top-talent in-house consulting team, to provide that support right from the start of the Baker-Polito administration. Members of the team would be deployed in groups of two or more to work on the most critical initiatives throughout state government. We would "physically" (pre-Covid) move these individuals to not only help provide the organizing structure, but also to be the heart of the dedicated team working the issue at the agency.

Strategic Ops was not a policy shop. Policy would be driven by other parts of the governor's office and the agencies. This team would be all about execution. Its members were recruited for their ability to bring immediate value-added skills, including data analysis, business process evaluation, metrics development, meeting facilitation, project management, and agile implementation. Previous government service was helpful but not a requirement. Team members were selected for their experience in getting things done in complex environments. Strategic Ops staffers would provide expertise that either didn't exist in the agency or was limited and severely stretched.

We know that in state government, accepting outside help is even more difficult for an agency leader when it comes from the governor's office. We understood that the idea of "help from the governor's office" would be a bit of an oxymoron for people accustomed to being on the receiving end of otherwise not-so-helpful calls. To make this work, we'd need a different kind of relationship between the executive office and the agency—not a top-down dynamic but an offer of service.

In our experience, this is flat-out different from the approach in other administrations. The traditional tendency of the executive office is to treat agency problems as public relations problems. Our focus is on *solving* the problems. The executive staff must work collaboratively and offer genuine value-added assistance. The leaders and agency staffers must be able to describe issues openly without fear of blame from the boss. It's a respectful partnership, a contribution of skills and resources to create an "us," not a "we-they," hyper-focused on improving the services government provides.

For every critical issue we tackled, a dedicated team was a requirement. It didn't have to be from the governor's office, but the team members had to be singularly devoted to the mission and have the experience, expertise, and ability to deliver. Never was this more important than with the Covid-19 pandemic. Health and Human Services Secretary Marylou Sudders was the dedicated leader of a core dedicated team staffed from various state agencies and supplemented by borrowed talent from private health-care organizations and consultants. And when we had specific, related problems to tackle—including food security, housing, contact tracing, and even reopening plans—we created additional dedicated teams.

How People Work Together

Working with others is essential for success in the public sector. In the private sector, within common rules and norms, the leaders of an organization can choose what to do, how to do it, when to do it, and whom to do it with. In the public sector—by design—the roles and responsibilities for setting direction and implementation are held by distinct entities that must work together for a successful outcome. This separation of powers is the basis of our democracy and a key to its endurance. Laws and budgets are the purview of the legislature; the delivery of services and the core functions of government are the responsibility of the administration; and sorting out disagreement over the intent of the law is the judiciary's role. In other words, one group decides how much to spend and what to spend it on, another implements, and the third serves as referee when necessary. Thus, in the public sector, the ability to work with others is not just important, it is how we *must* work.

Four qualities create a foundation for achieving results: trust, humility, respect, and compromise.

Trust requires constant action, continual dialogue, and core respect. It means creating an environment of active listening and asking questions. It means sharing knowledge and accepting that it's OK to say what's not working. It is being open to describing risks. It is taking responsibility and being a partner. Trust means honoring intent through implementation and action. It is earned and tested.

Humility comes from lessons learned over time. It is knowing that you don't have all the answers and that there's more than one way to do something. It is recognizing that others have knowledge, experience, and wisdom that you do not. It comes from the realization that you will make mistakes and will need the courage to acknowledge and learn from them.

Respect is a mutual act that enables and provides confidence. It creates a basis for engagement. It provides a platform for divergent views and for an environment where the sum can be greater than its parts. It means that hate, bigotry, and violence are not to be tolerated and must be condemned. Respect is essential to build bridges that create results.

Compromise comes from an understanding that we all have different life experiences, perspectives, and interests. It acknowledges that there are multiple ways to achieve the same end and multiple steps along the way. Compromise recognizes not only specific interests, but also the interests of the whole community. It can be the forerunner of progress in breaking the rigidity of "all or nothing" and the gridlock that may ensue.

Bridgewater State: A hospital in name only

The effort to improve long-standing poor conditions and services at Bridgewater State Hospital provides a good example of how to work effectively with others. The issue didn't have an impact on a lot of people, but for those who were affected, the consequences were too often deeply troubling. In 2016, a year after taking office, a patient's death there punctuated why change was needed.

In the Massachusetts prison system, Bridgewater State Hospital is for men with severe mental illness who have committed a crime. Some of the most troubled men in the state live there in a highly secure facility. In 2016, Bridgewater was a hospital in name only. Surrounded by high fences and barbed wire, it focused on security, not on providing mental health services to those with significant needs.

Those needs and inadequate services created constant tension between the staff and patients. The result for patients was an extensive use of physical restraints and long periods of seclusion. Not a prescription for success for people with mental illness.

Bridgewater put a long-standing stain on how the Commonwealth treated some of its most vulnerable. In 1967, Frederick Wiseman made a documentary film, *Titicut Follies*, about the despair and conditions at the hospital. The film portrayed the often-unbathed occupants of Bridgewater State Hospital, holed up in empty cells. It also showed patients required to strip naked publicly and be force-fed. The hospital staff had an attitude that ranged from indifference to outright abuse. The film was censored by the government of Massachusetts. Twenty years later, in 1987, the *New York Times* noted that this was "the only American film ever censored for reasons other than obscenity or national security."[2] The article continued, reporting that the conditions at the hospital had improved since the film, but for us this wasn't enough.

In the decades since 1987, the issues at Bridgewater had never been fully attended to. I was determined to see if the conditions at the facility could be addressed. I charged three of my cabinet secretaries, Daniel Bennett (public safety), Marylou Sudders (health and human services), and Kristen Lepore (administration and finance), with taking this on. A dedicated team that included staffers from each of the secretariats was formed to support the effort.

Working with others would be essential. Bridgewater had three significant constituencies: (1) patients' families and legal advocacy groups, (2) the staff and its union, and (3) the state legislature (for funding). My cabinet secretaries would work with each group.

An evening meeting with patient advocates and their families, attended by Steve and secretaries Bennett and Sudders, provided a breakthrough for the whole effort. Never before had so much attention been focused on this issue. Marylou was well known and respected in the mental health community as the former commissioner of mental health and an ongoing patients' rights advocate. Many of those attending knew her, which established a basic level of trust for the meeting. Daniel Bennett was in charge of the Department of Corrections, the agency responsible for Bridgewater. His team knew how to run safe prison systems. Steve's presence signaled that this was a priority for the governor.

For a couple of hours, the administration's team listened and learned. Within a few weeks, in response to the families, some modest changes in visitation policy were made. However, they didn't constitute what anyone would call success. A peer comparison proved crucial in making changes at the hospital. When we compared the services provided at Bridgewater with those at facilities with similar populations in other states, we found Bridgewater to be an outlier— and not in a positive way. That comparison led our team to rethink the model of care at Bridgewater.

The multipart plan for intervention included a significant change in the roles of the staff, including correction officers and mental health professionals. Corrections had responsibility for providing security, yet its staff was involved in mental health activities throughout the facility. These people were trained security professionals, not mental health service providers. Under the new model, corrections officers would do what they did best, and trained health professionals would do what they did best. Overall, this meant decreasing corrections personnel and increasing mental health personnel. Among the former, the fear of job loss was palpable.

Honest dialogue and a measure of trust between Secretary Bennett and the Massachusetts Correction Officers Federated Union proved pivotal. Their discussions focused on what this change would mean not only at Bridgewater but also for the whole corrections system. Ultimately, working closely with the union, Dan worked out a way to prevent job loss by transferring some Bridgewater corrections staffers to open positions in other department locations. To provide expanded mental health services, a new vendor whose experience incorporated the best elements of the peer study was engaged, with guidance from Marylou. Finally, Kristen worked with the legislature to secure funding for a transition to the new service model.

The outcomes have been remarkable. As reported in the *Boston Globe* in September 2017, "At Last, Decency at Bridgewater. . . . The staff has cut seclusion of patients by 99 percent, and the practice of strapping them down by 98 percent. The facility now functions more like an actual hospital."[3]

Having leaders with the ability to work with others meant that the interests of the patients' families and legal advocates, corrections staffers and their union, and the legislature were brought together for a positive result. And it required trust, humility, respect, and compromise from all.

Working *with*, not working *at*

We're not being Pollyannas. We understand that differences between positions and personalities may prove too much to overcome. We respect organizational boundaries and the division of authority among governmental branches required by the Constitution. But results come when we are talking *with*, not *at*, one another. Working together creates a sum greater than the parts. It can result in breakthroughs and significant improvement in performance. Working at odds with one another creates we-they, winners-losers, division, and turf battles. There have been too many examples of this in Washington. Working *with* can bring about positive change; working *at* is often not just neutral but actually negative. It creates collateral damage.

Our greatest frustration has come when we've been unable to find common ground among stakeholders on a critical topic. Just saying no may make a point, but it effectively means no progress, no change. It's easier to point fingers than to do the hard work together to make something happen. As Teddy Roosevelt said, "It's not the critic who counts." It's about "the man [woman] who is actually in the arena."

Our public schools have provided an example during Covid-19 of how important it is to work *with*, and how easy it is to fall into working *at*. Some twenty-plus years ago, a great coming together of people from across political perspectives created a landmark education-reform package that vaulted Massachusetts to the top in the nation's K–12 performance. But through Covid-19, oftentimes, it seemed we were working at odds with one another—and the collateral damage was to our children. While there was broad agreement on many items regarding the health and safety of our students, teachers, and staff, the approach of the teachers' union leadership was troubling. For the fall of 2020, most of the teachers' union leaders seemed opposed to many reasonable attempts to open our schools for in-person learning, despite the assurances and the appeals of the medical community.

I don't believe that this can be written off as a Republican governor versus a union. Not in Massachusetts. Not with me. Working with Service Employees International Union 509 was critical to the improvements needed at the Department of Children and Families. Working with the Boston Carmen's Union was critical to the comeback of bus and train services at the Massachusetts Bay Transportation Authority after devasting winter storms. Collaboration with the Massachusetts Correction Officers Federated Union created a win-win for Bridgewater patients and staff. During Covid, the unions representing the staff of legal aid organizations agreed to expedite hiring processes in order to provide prompt legal services in the courts for those facing housing eviction.

As the pandemic has progressed, I hope that we will have worked this out for our schoolchildren. With Covid-19, there were so many positive examples of working together. This one bothers me deeply, especially because of its impact on our kids.

Avoiding turf battles

In any administration, potential turf battles and conflict are innate and natural. They need to be addressed directly, starting at the top. I saw firsthand that the most-successful administrations are those that are aware of and address these latent organizational battle-grounds. Otherwise, turf battles can wreak havoc, especially for a new administration.

While personnel appointments were of utmost importance, how we organized the governor's office would determine whether the result was a bunch of individuals or a functioning team. To reinforce the concept of the governor and the lieutenant governor as one team, we would have a single office structure, with the chief of staff and all functions serving both Karyn and me. We would have weekly cabinet meetings. For other discussions, I wanted the relevant sec-retary and agency leaders and key members of the governor's office staff to attend.

We would come to know and work with one another. Face-to-face (pre-Covid) in the room together. Common space for common ground. Building respect, relationships, and results. A turf tamp-down.

I believe that being in this together allowed us to tackle a huge budget deficit, snow emergencies, and other complex problems not as isolated actions but as a strong team effort. We had five years of practice at this before Covid-19. As a result, we could act quickly as a team. Problem-solving across agencies. Lending staff members to one another. Quickly sharing best practices and materials.

As you will see in the coming chapters, "people are policy" affects every part of the Results Framework, so spend time at the beginning to get this right. It allows the best shot at success. It is not about partisanship; it is about performance. It is not about who you know; it is about know-how. It is not about isolated actions and divisive rhetoric; it is about the power of *we*.

Follow the Facts

Karyn Polito and I had just finished up several meetings with local leaders in western Massachusetts. This was spring 2016. Their frustration had reached the boiling point over a topic that I hadn't expected—the internet. Sharing a border with New York and Vermont, this was a place of small village centers, individual households, and farms tucked in the hills of fifty-three towns in three western Massachusetts counties. The lack of reliable, affordable internet was affecting everyone. Small shops were unable to fulfill online orders. Inns couldn't quickly respond to reservation requests. Dial-up service crashed on a busy night at a restaurant, bollixing up dinner for customers and staffers alike. Parents had to park their cars outside locations with hot spots so that their kids could complete homework. Families were unable to sell their homes. An unreliable internet meant disrupted daily routines, business losses, depressed real estate prices, and, in some cases, unintended isolation.

One after another, the people Karyn and I spoke with described not only the very real impact on their lives and livelihood, but also their disaffection with government. I could hear in their voices that they viewed us as just another bunch of Boston politicians who didn't understand—or didn't care about—western Massachusetts, especially the hill towns. Our citizens were saying, in their own way and words, "If you really cared about us, you would fix this. Now."

If you live or work in Massachusetts, one of the technology leaders of the world, it may be hard to imagine not having reliable internet service for your home or business. But as Karyn and I heard loud and clear, for many communities in western Massachusetts, that was the case, even after the state had launched the Massachusetts Broadband Initiative with some $50 million in funding a decade earlier.

The initiative had money, a staff, and a clear mission. Yet after ten years and nearly $10 million spent, it had little to show. The successful building out of the so-called middle mile was an important step. That technology pipeline allowed internet service for bigger businesses and entities such as hospitals and universities that were within range and could afford the sizable investment to connect with this new infrastructure. However, for the typical household or small business, broadband internet was a promise unfulfilled. The human stories were impossible to ignore. "Frustration" was the polite word for what people felt.

We had inherited the Massachusetts Broadband Initiative from the previous administration. Now it was ours. Rural internet access moved to the top of the list of problems Karyn and I wanted to fix. As far as we were concerned, internet service was fundamental infrastructure, as important as running water and electricity.

We asked Jay Ash, our secretary of housing and economic development, to prioritize this issue. Jay had been the city manager of Chelsea, a small urban center just north of Boston. He grew up in the Chelsea housing projects, got a basketball scholarship to Clark University in Worcester, worked in the legislature, and then found himself back in Chelsea, working to improve the place where he grew up. As city manager, Jay had been successful in attracting new development and jobs to this struggling low-income community.

I picked Jay for his cabinet role for his knowledge and know-how. He had demonstrated how municipalities could get things done. A keen observer of people and places, he understood the reality of US House Speaker Tip O'Neill's words "All politics is local" and what that meant for those western Massachusetts communities.

Jay called for an immediate review of the broadband initiative. Understanding the criticality of people are policy, he named a former state representative from the area as the initiative's new board chair and recruited a well-regarded community planner based in western Massachusetts as the day-to-day liaison. Immediately, their expertise added credibility to the policy effort that had felt out of touch with those it was attempting to serve. From the governor's office, staffers from the Strategic Ops and legal teams would provide organizing support and strategic advice. This group would work with the existing staff to reset the effort.

Clearly, we'd identified a major problem. But what were the facts? Understanding them was essential to the design and implementation of any successful intervention. The follow-the-facts review showed an implementation model that just wasn't working after ten years. The Massachusetts Broadband Initiative was failing at every level:

- **Customer:** Individuals, families, and businesses were without internet connectivity.

- **Town:** Unworkable plans had been developed for each town to deliver this key service.

- **Initiative as a whole:** A lot of activity and spending had occurred, with little to show for it.

The initiative had launched in 2006. In 2016, of the fifty-three communities targeted, nine had limited service and forty-four had none.

Go Hard at the Facts

To get at the facts, we conducted a detailed review for each town that included data on population size, municipal finances, the number of homes and businesses to be reached, and how difficult it would be to make the actual connections.

These facts established an early estimate of the potential cost to implement and then run the internet service. As part of the fact analysis, the team also reviewed the grant-award rules and found them so onerous as to be nearly impossible for the communities to follow. For these difficult-to-serve communities of diverse wealth and dispersed population, the one-size-fits-all approach was rigid and bureaucratic. The focus seemed to be on following the process rather than delivering the service. It was not surprising that thousands of people and hundreds of businesses were still underserved.

The team followed the facts to zero in on these problems and then determine what to do about them and how to do it. In a matter of weeks, it developed a multipronged implementation plan. For immediate impact, the Broadband Extension Program was launched to leverage the relationship with existing internet service providers in the nine towns that had limited service. In those communities, the telecommunications companies agreed to rapidly mobilize crews to prioritize the internet expansion; the towns agreed to expedite any zoning and related approvals; and the Boston-based team supplied legal support and funds to bridge the financing gap. What had previously felt like a series of stone walls became path-building public-private partnerships.

Within two years, internet service had been provided to more than a thousand homes and businesses. As reported by the *Springfield Republican*, "The towns of Buckland, Chester, Conway, Hardwick,

Huntington, Montague, Northfield, Pelham and Shelburne now have vastly expanded internet access. . . . Comcast had previously deemed it uneconomic to provide service to most areas of the rural towns, but the company agreed to expand its cable network to 1,089 new premises with a $4 million grant from the state."[1]

Think options, not a single solution

For the other forty-four towns, the team looked at the facts that were preventing progress. Each community differed in population size and density, financial or bonding capability, and topography. Community leaders had varying ideas about the type of service needed and who would own and operate it. As the team picked through these specific facts, it picked apart the idea of a single approach, designing five models from which each community could choose. The menu of options presented a range of public-private partnerships, technology, and financing solutions. Instead of Boston dictating exactly how things would be done, each community was empowered to determine the most appropriate option. The Boston-based team would provide technical support and streamline the financial grant program.

A town could choose to work with a telecommunications provider such as Comcast or Verizon, to extend the service from a nearby community to its own municipality. Other options leveraged local and regional players, such as a relatively new service, Whip City Fiber. The town of Westfield, which was called Whip City because of a history of manufacturing horsewhips, was one of about a dozen communities in Massachusetts with its own municipal power utility. Westfield Gas and Electric provided internet through its subsidiary, Whip City Fiber. The small town of Rowe was a happy example of the twenty or so towns that picked it to provide internet service. In

August 2019, Whip City Fiber proclaimed: "Rowe leaps across the digital divide. A month ago, Rowe ranked among the bottom 5 percent of the country for internet connection speeds. Now it's in the top 5 percent. Customers report having speeds that are literally hundreds of times faster than with the previously available DSL."[2]

Soon internet services were being planned or underway in more than forty of the fifty-three target communities. At the customer level, this meant that thousands of individuals, families, and businesses would be able to stream, search, and otherwise fully participate in the digital world. At the town level, the five-model approach offered options that worked. And on the overall organizational level, the state broadband initiative was fulfilling its promise.

Adjust according to facts on the ground

Once significant progress was achieved, we conducted a follow-up fact review. It revealed that a key obstacle to ensuring internet service in all fifty-three communities was funding. The $40 million that remained from the original 2006 funding was big, but not big enough to complete the work. Nearly every project was more complex, the geography more difficult, and the money required more than what had been conceived a decade earlier. Successful implementation meant adequately funding each project, not trying to spread the dollars in such a way that all might have a piece of the pie but no one project would succeed. We were determined not to proceed on a first-come, first-served basis, which would block access to some communities. The point of the program was to provide service to all fifty-three targeted towns. The legislature agreed. In November 2017, eighteen months after we began to tackle the rural internet issue, I signed legislation to provide an additional $45 million to close the high-speed broadband internet gap in those communities.

Still, some communities could not find a partner. For the hill towns in particular, a small population and large distances between homes made it difficult to find providers to install and operate the service. After discussion with possible telecommunication partners and community leaders, we learned that a key stumbling block was the Broadband Initiative's own contractual time limit related to connecting 96 percent of customers in a community. Allowing some latitude on that point could benefit both the communities and the providers.

The team proposed this among other minor policy changes—and it worked. These modifications exemplified an approach that makes adjustments according to the facts on the ground. On January 22, 2018, a headline in the *Berkshire Eagle* announced: "Last of 'last mile' towns now have broadband suitors. The small rural town of Florida had been working for over 8 years to bring internet access to its residents. Christine Dobbert, the town's administrator, proclaimed, 'Today, with four broadband suitors, Florida no longer stands alone at a digital altar. Now we're just trying to pick one.'"[3]

As of fall 2021, fifty of the fifty-three rural towns have new service, and the remaining three are in various phases of implementation. For the hamlet of Mount Washington, with just 150 households, the change wasn't only about the internet. As told to *Government Technology*, Brian Tobin, a select board member, observed, "In the 13 years before we had high-speed Internet, there wasn't a single child born to any couple in the town of Mount Washington. In two years, five children have been born, and new couples have moved in. So, I don't know what I would attribute to broadband or anything else, but I can tell you it's a big difference in a small community where we were losing population as older folks passed on."[4]

Following the facts propelled an evaluation of the initial program failures, proved instrumental in the new program design, and determined what changes were needed for ultimate success. In other words, the data and the stories drove us to focus on the problem to solve and therefore be specific about what to do and how to do it.

Gather Evidence and Uncover Points of Pain

Coming into government with a belief that we could do things better, I was interested in what the data actually showed. Understanding the data and not just a program's intent really mattered. Data points. Context. What is the size of the problem? How long has the problem persisted? Do we know what the initial causes might be and what happened in the environment to allow this condition to persist or get worse? How many people are affected? Is there a breakdown by customer? What are the trends? What is the current context? What is the legal and regulatory framework? What do the financials look like? What are the year-over-year numbers? What are the seasonal trends? Was there a critical event that served as a trigger? How have others handled this? What are the leading concepts in this area? I was always burning with questions that seemed critical to achieve a baseline of understanding.

Beyond the data, I wanted to know what was happening to the people served by these programs and the providers of the service. How did clients describe what was broken? What was it like to go through the process? What was the impact on their lives, businesses, communities? What were service providers and administrators of the program saying were the problems?

Following the facts provides oxygen to the Results Framework. Facts are not abstract; they are explicit. Concentrate on the facts that lead to a sharp understanding of the problems to be solved and a clear direction for addressing them. Be skeptical. Be hard on the facts. And above all, don't use only the facts you like and exclude others. Unbiased and objective, the facts we follow provide an understanding of the present reality, stimulate the development of new options, and set a baseline for measuring the impact of the change initiative.

We follow two types of facts: *data evidence* and *points of pain*. Data evidence refers to snapshots of current programs and their status, including items that can be described quantitatively and qualitatively. It includes number and type of staffers, revenue and operating costs, technical and paper processes, and program elements such as eligibility and approvals. We also look to this detailed information to understand underlying economic factors, historical program trends, and what others have done or are considering to address similar problems. For us, data evidence provides the basic details and numbers underpinning a change effort. All the essential information must be not only assembled but, most important, analyzed at the individual transaction level, the program level, and for trends.

Points of pain are the second part of the fact set we follow. There are many ways to begin to understand a problem. With points of pain, we gather specific stories about specific incidents to move the problem from an academic paper, a number, or a systems hiccup to something that is tangible and human. Personal anecdotes tell us what is broken and needs to be fixed. They suggest solutions for what needs to be fixed in ways that the aggregate data alone does not.

Taken together, data evidence and points of pain offer a mind-and-heart perspective on what needs to change. As an effort begins, this view of the facts creates a common platform for leadership and the team to determine what problem needs solving and provide direction for the design and implementation of policy and program interventions to fix it. In sum, start with the facts on the ground as they are, devise and implement interventions intended to improve them, and measure the facts all along the way.

Get Out of the Tower

Tips Tools and Tactics

Go beyond the boundaries of an organization in order to learn—breaking the information bubble that can form around a leader. Organizations tend to turn inward when they need to turn outward. *Getting out of the tower* is about building new knowledge and greater capacity by reaching beyond the data at hand. Think of it as a quiet assault on the status quo.

- **Get out of the office.** Talk to all types of people directly—those impacted by a change, those providing goods and services, as well as key constituencies, advocates, and, especially in the making of public policy, legislators.

- **Get out beyond internal reports.** Cull information from outside experts, seek comparative performance data, and constantly review articles and reports.

- **Get out to make site visits.** Go to a local office to see how things work. Meet the tech team, the group processing

Registry of Motor Vehicles

Our approach toward following facts—find them, acknowledge them, and then use them to address the problems—works when facts are findable, or when they are not overlooked, hidden, or intentionally buried. An experience with the Registry of Motor Vehicles illustrates how not having the facts can lead to disastrous results.

applications, and any service team in the location. Meet with these key staff members, solicit their input, and take in their work environment.

- **Get out for the customer experience.** Take on the role of customer, the person receiving the service, or the customer who wants to. When you and team members go through the process—from filling out a form to receiving the service itself—you see the problems and imagine needs to be addressed.

- **Get out to talk to peers.** Unlike the private sector, with its trade secrets and instinct to protect competitive advantage, your peers in other towns, cities, states, and other jurisdictions typically want to help and are ready to describe what worked and what didn't.

- **Get out to local universities.** Local colleges and universities are unrecognized resources. Engage the faculty with expertise and the students who want to help solve public-sector problems.

- **Get out again and again.** Make it a regular practice.

On June 21, 2019, a dreadful accident took the lives of seven people. A pickup truck with a trailer crossed over the yellow line on Route 2 in Randolph, New Hampshire, and collided with a group of motorcyclists. The truck driver, Volodymr Zhukovskyy, twenty-three, was intoxicated. Worse, he was driving with a license that should have already been terminated. The Registry of Motor Vehicles had received a notice in May from the State of Connecticut indicating that he had been charged with drunk driving. The notice was read by Registry staff, but no action taken. An investigation that followed revealed that this was one of thousands of licenses that should have been questioned or suspended. There were literally dozens of boxes and bins of these notices that for years had been simply stacked in the Registry offices.

For years, not much had happened with these notices at the Registry, and there appeared to be few consequences. But not this time. Lives were lost. Investigations commenced. During the months leading up to this fatal incident, the Registry had been in the midst of a major overhaul of its customer services, including its operations and tech systems. There were regular forums where all kinds of problems were being raised and then addressed. It didn't happen this time. When the facts finally surfaced, disaster had already struck.

The fact that these notices had been ignored, that they had not been unearthed, led to a management overhaul. A new leader was named, and a better process of self-scrutiny instituted. The new team quickly tackled the problem, revoking the permission to drive a vehicle from more than 5,200 individuals.

I wouldn't say that this incident is a case in which our framework failed. You can't follow the facts if you don't have them. But government leaders must never make excuses. The question for a leader becomes, how do you discover the unknown? How do you uncover dismaying facts lurking in bureaucracies when, thousands of times before, there appeared no material consequences? How can facts be revealed before they lead to tragedy?

Any loss of life is tragic. One that could be avoided perhaps more so. I was deeply saddened by the Route 2 accident and all that we learned in its wake. We can't go back and undo what's been done, but we can take action to prevent such lapses.

Leaders can and must create environments where both good news and bad news can be raised. As difficult as it may be for the leaders to hear bad news, it is perhaps more difficult for staff to bring up— especially after a tragedy, a mishap, or a moment when systems aren't working. These messengers should be praised. It's their message that we should focus on, and fix.

The opioid epidemic

In 2015, opioids were a public health crisis that crisscrossed the entire state and yet was being neither discussed nor addressed. The epidemic, more than twenty years in the making, was snowballing. The number of opioid-related deaths was exploding. Family members and neighbors were dying in nearly every community across the state, and there was no end in sight.

This problem had no simple solution. Opioid-related addiction and deaths, though evident in every state, were not yet a national issue. While we prided ourselves on being number one on many matters, from education to health-care access, it turned out that Massachusetts was also number one in opioid overdoses. Only a few other states had begun to confront the issue. I wanted to know what treatment programs helped. What could be done to prevent these numbers from increasing? What was the data showing? What was the state of services in Massachusetts? What were the best practices? How could we effectively implement them? We needed a comprehensive approach that started with *people* and *facts*.

In February, I formed the Governor's Opioid Working Group, to be led by Secretary of Health and Human Services Marylou Sudders, to address the crisis. The group's eighteen members represented the judiciary, local officials, medical experts, law enforcement, and the head of the AFL-CIO. An estimated 978 people had died of

Round the Table

An effective tool to get to all corners, *round the table* is a frank assessment, even a call to air dirty laundry. This discussion happens ideally as part of an initiative's kickoff—a critical moment to identify problems or name the crisis and establish key facts. As these can be difficult conversations, certain techniques are helpful.

A meeting facilitator literally goes around the room and asks each person to speak—regardless of position or title. The twin goals are to surface important perspectives and to get all participants to speak, listen, and be heard without judgment. One by one, each person has a moment to ask a question, provide a clarification, indicate an important fact, or make any other relevant comment to the work at hand.

While we have used this approach to get at the facts, the round-the-table is a method that subtly upends the status quo. It helps create engagement and clarity. The typical meeting agenda doesn't allow for this open discussion. Build it in! This practice can close a meeting or it can be invoked multiples times during one. Here are some tried-and-true steps for facilitators:

- Note that the leader or department head speaks first, then everyone is expected to say a few words.

- Ask the leader for opening observations about the major concerns to address.

- Seek volunteers to comment next. After a few have spoken, then direct the conversation to go around the room in order of seating, so that everyone participates.

- Encourage each participant to describe what they believe are key points of pain. They can speak from their own perspective or what they have heard from others.

- State that it is OK to bring up other problems—as well as ideas to tackle the concerns raised.

- Remind the group that hearing a variety of perspectives can be cathartic—and also sometimes overwhelming.

- Capture critical information, specific points of pain, and proposed solutions.

- Close with a summary, including assignments and next steps.

The act of going around the room is a great equalizer. It surfaces what people are truly thinking, it gets facts out in the open, and it allows the group to build a common understanding. As you and the team go forward, use this practice to ground the specifics of problems to solve and effective means to do so. Consider the specific points of pain uncovered as part of the performance metrics.

opioid-related overdoses in Massachusetts in 2013—46 percent more than the year before. I charged the group with taking a no-holds-barred approach to the crisis.

This was not a partisan matter. I wanted Steve Tolman, president of the AFL-CIO, to have a big voice in the group. Yes, he was the most prominent labor leader in the state, a former legislator, and a Democrat. More important, Tolman understood the pain and suffering of the men and women and their families who had been affected by this epidemic. While nobody expected us to agree on lots of things, he and I had met periodically throughout the recent gubernatorial campaign to discuss this issue. No one was a more passionate fighter.

On June 22, 2015, I announced the working group's recommendations. Taking action on the opioid crisis was one of my top priorities, and this was my first major announcement about what we were prepared to do. Room 157, the press room on the first floor of the statehouse, was packed with reporters, microphones, and TV cameras.

The working group's report was deep, comprehensive, and grounded in facts. We needed to understand the history, the data, and the trends here in Massachusetts and across the nation. The working group had compiled the data evidence—a review of the academic research, government reports, and the reports of previous task forces and commissions. It had examined documents and recommendations sent by more than 150 organizations. Further, it had held listening sessions across the state to hear directly from those affected by the epidemic. In the end, more than 1,100 Massachusetts residents made their voices heard. Opioids and heroin were affecting people of all ages, from newborns with addiction passed along through birth, to young athletes and older patients trying to manage pain and then finding themselves addicted. The crisis was felt in homes, among health-care providers, and in the child-welfare system.

From this comprehensive fact set—data evidence and points of pain—the working group distilled findings into four critical areas: prevention, intervention, treatment, and recovery support. It made sixty-five recommendations about what to do and outlined how to do it. Each recommendation indicated who would be responsible for implementation, through either administrative or legislative action. The report became a blueprint for a multiyear approach to addressing this crisis.

After the report's release, we took action on many of the recommendations. In the months that followed, a new system for tracking prescriptions was implemented, hundreds of new treatment beds were set up, federal and state funding for support groups increased, and strong prevention and education programs got underway. We made much progress, but our review of the facts showed that several key legislative interventions were still needed.

On March 14, 2016, a little more than one year after launching the effort, Karyn and I stood at the base of the grand staircase in the statehouse with the members of the working group. We were flanked by the House speaker, the Senate president, the attorney general, and dozens of others as I signed into law a comprehensive bill aimed at changing the trajectory of the epidemic. It included several first-in-the-nation proposals, such as a limit on first-time prescriptions of seven days, to address the rampant supply of opioids, and it required training for medical and social service professionals. After signing the bill, as I stood at the podium, I found myself in tears as I recalled the stories of men and women and their families struggling with drug addiction. The crowd began to clap, giving me a chance to compose myself before going on with my remarks. At the time, I thought about how often blue-ribbon groups never amount to much. There's fanfare at the proclamation and then quiet. But this group came together and delivered. My words would not be as important, or as well remembered, as this collective action.

Within a year, we started to see some positive changes. Opioid prescriptions were dropping significantly. New regulation made Narcan, a kind of miracle antidote to an overdose, widely available. Education programs were in place, not only for health-care providers, but also for high school athletes and their families. We had new tools to fight fentanyl, the latest scourge of the epidemic.

Perhaps most significant, for the first time, opioid-related overdose deaths decreased year over year. The Department of Public Health's third-quarter report showed that they had declined by an estimated 10 percent in the first nine months of 2017. Our new laws and programs became models for other states and for the nation.

By February 2019, Department of Public Health studies showed that the number of people who died from opioid-related overdoses had dropped 4 percent in 2018—the second consecutive year to show a drop. Still too many deaths and lives harmed. But prevention efforts were beginning to pay dividends. More treatment options provided immediate care.

In a short time, with this fact-based approach—defining the problem and then focusing on appropriate intervention—much progress was made. As we write in the fall of 2021, opioid overdoses and deaths have climbed across the nation not only because of the devastating impact of fentanyl, but also because of the specific consequences of Covid, limiting facility care capacity and face-to-face support. In Massachusetts, while seeing some increase, the total number of fatalities stabilized over the past two years and was still lower than at the peak in 2016. However, the impact was greatest in communities of color. While the Commonwealth has significantly increased its investments in prevention and care, we recognize that there's much more to do.

. . .

In sum, following the facts provides the foundational information—data evidence and points of pain—for the Results Framework. It means being objective, learning from others, and uncovering the human stories. It means both going deep into the data and revealing the real on-the-ground impact. It's about recognizing what is there, not just what you want to see. While there is always more to learn, we do not let the perfect be the enemy of the good. The facts are not an end unto themselves. We follow the facts to define the problem to address and imagine the activities and actions to resolve them.

Focus on How

f I had to sum up the past year in office in one phrase," I said in my first State of the Commonwealth address, "it would be the following: don't be surprised when you get surprised." I was referring to the series of devastating storms in 2015 that had shut down the state for weeks, the extent of the opioid epidemic, the size of the budget deficit, and a list of other problems that kept coming.

At the start of my sixth year as governor, in 2020, I kept thinking that no matter how many times I told myself to expect the unexpected, I could never have imagined what would be visited upon us. Covid-19 was not just an unanticipated event. It was a *behemoth* of the unexpected—a pandemic on a scale not seen in a hundred years. On March 20, the first death from the virus occurred in Massachusetts. At that time, it was impossible to envision how many others would shortly follow. In the twenty years from 1955 to 1975, just over 1,300 Massachusetts residents died in the Vietnam War. Every death mattered. But in just twenty months from March 2020 to November 2021 with the pandemic still in our midst, the Covid fatalities reported in Massachusetts would total nearly fifteen times that number. We lost 19,000 family members, neighbors, and friends.

In the early weeks of March, I had declared a state of emergency and established a government-wide command center. Marylou

Sudders was the lead. Making the announcement is one thing, and it's critically important. But making it work is the nut to crack. While *people are policy* is the overarching theme that unifies all the steps, and *follow the facts* is a key pillar of the Results Framework, *focus on how* is the engine to achieving the goals of each initiative. As with any other complex and significant effort, Marylou and her dedicated teams would spend the most time and resources to focus on how. Marylou's obsession with the practical realities of moving a concept to results was a key reason I had chosen her to lead the Covid-19 response. Whether the goal was to increase testing, ensure hospital bed capacity, address the personal protective equipment shortage, or provide contact tracing, attention to the what and the how of implementation was the linchpin for a successful outcome.

Covid-19: Setting up a Statewide Effort

One evening in late March 2020, I arrived at home and sat in the car to take a call with Marylou, Steve, and Jim Kim, the former head of the World Bank and global health expert. Steve and I had been in touch earlier in the week, when it had become clear that an expanded contact-tracing effort would be critical. On this call, Jim was going to describe what he was hearing from former colleagues around the world about the pandemic in general and contact tracing in particular.

Contact tracing involves reaching out to people who have been exposed to someone with an infectious disease to let them and their own close contacts know so that they can protect themselves and others and prevent further spread of the disease. It's a basic public health practice that has been used successfully in the United States and across the globe for decades.

Jim explained what he had learned directly from experts at the World Health Organization and in South Korea and other nations. He talked about the need for the prevention, testing, care, and isolation efforts that were just getting underway and described the importance of contact tracing to mitigate transmission.

After Jim spoke, we talked for another ten minutes about a concept he was proposing: a virtual, remote phone-bank operation of contact tracers who would reach out to people who had tested positive for Covid-19. The one-on-one outreach would provide key information about Covid-19 and its symptoms, offer support to isolate safely, and alert the person's close contacts. The program could be scaled up or down to meet the need statewide and to support each city or town's local contact-tracing efforts. "Let's go," I said. "This is the first thing I've heard that may give us a way to attack this damn thing." Marylou agreed.

As with other critical initiatives, we began by discussing several immediate recommendations for the team to succeed. The first would be to engage Louis Gutierrez as the managerial lead. Louis was currently running the Massachusetts Health Connector, the state's Obamacare health insurance exchange. Although this would be an additional responsibility, getting Gutierrez involved meant benefiting from his proven understanding of the interrelationship of technology and operations and of the people, budget, and legal support it takes to implement a complex system. At its core, the contact-tracing effort was all about systems and their effective operations.

Second, retain Partners In Health to do the actual contact tracing and an experienced consultant to set up and manage the Collaborative's data information system. Partners In Health, based in Boston, is internationally recognized for its work fighting malaria, tuberculosis, HIV/AIDS, and Ebola in some of the toughest places in the world. For those engagements, the organization literally wrote the book on contact tracing and community support.

Third, ensure that the Department of Public Health was a founding partner in this initiative, as the agency managing the state's disease surveillance, tracking, and reporting. Working closely with local boards of health, the department would ensure a common approach for all efforts related to contact tracing.

Marylou designated a liaison from the command center to what we soon called the Community Tracing Collaborative.

By statute, the Department of Public Health and each municipality's local board of health were responsible for contact tracing. The Community Tracing Collaborative was established to supplement and support the efforts of those 351 boards, ranging from small-town volunteers to big-city public health departments. The boards have a broad agenda in normal times, and their responsibilities deepened with the pandemic. Under the Community Tracing Collaborative, each local board could choose when (all the time, weekends only, surge moments) and how (every case, cluster investigation, cross-jurisdictional) it would opt in for help.

The key information from following the facts was clear: (1) the number of positive Covid-19 tests was rising geometrically, and (2) local health boards and staffers were limited in their ability to reach everyone. And although "only" hundreds of new cases were being identified each day, we expected that soon thousands of individuals and households would be affected. For the Community Tracing Collaborative, the problem to solve was achieving outreach to positive cases and their contacts in a timely, effective way. "Timely" was not just an adjective; it was the key measure of success in mitigating further transmission.

We knew from experience that setting up something this extraordinary in just a few weeks would require an organized approach and a dedicated staff. We immediately embedded a project-management function at the heart and start of this new operation.

In the days that followed, the Tracing Collaborative's core team put together a more fully developed proposal and budget: this was our *what to do*. The plan was to establish a virtual call center of more than a thousand contact tracers, staffed by Partners In Health and using a sophisticated customer-relations-management technology platform that interfaced with the state's epidemiologic tracking system. The Department of Public Health would provide overall guidance, approve all protocols, and be a critical connection to local public health agencies. Project management would be provided by a central team out of the Health Connector. The last step was to set a target time frame for having the first staffers hired and trained, making the base system operational, and making the first calls. The target? Two weeks.

Now resources, time, and energy would shift from what to do to *how to do it*. How to set up a working call center, hire more than a thousand callers, develop protocols, and ensure accurate links to the epidemiology tracking system. In short order, we would go from a central team of a dozen or so to a team of hundreds.

Community Tracing Collaborative

Project management would be critical. We quickly broke down the total effort into work streams that included specific projects and other key tasks with target time frames. They were focused on call-center operations, protocols and training, technology development, data and reporting, and communications. Each part of the initiative had an accountable leader and team with a deadline to meet.

Meetings to check in on overall progress were held twice daily, one at 7:45 a.m. and the other at 4:30 p.m. The early-morning meeting was a recap of the work of the previous evening; it identified key issues to address in the day ahead. One by one, the work streams' leaders would report on progress, problems, and performance metrics. Adjustments were made quickly. The late-afternoon meeting provided specific updates and was often used for deeper problem-solving sessions. Other meetings were held throughout the day and into the evening.

It was an intense and sometimes jarring effort, but in twelve days, we started making the first calls to Covid-19-positive individuals. In a few weeks, more than a thousand newly hired callers were conducting this critical one-to-one outreach. Each call required an ability to convey information regarding Covid-19, explain the status of the individual's case, describe next steps to isolate or quarantine, and identify close contacts to prevent further transmission.

During the spring, the Community Tracing Collaborative grew from a rough-and-tumble startup into a more mature, albeit young, organization working through its growing pains. The strong project-management approach and attention to performance metrics allowed the core team members to quickly understand progress and make necessary adjustments where there were problems. For example, when the number of people reached by callers was lower than expected, the team devised a media and outreach campaign—Answer the Call—and implemented an automated text message with a number to call at the Community Tracing Collaborative.

Data and reporting issues were another example. They were initially handled as one-off items, and it soon became clear that they needed more attention. A Solutions Priority Council was established to ensure appropriate prioritization, coordination, and testing of changes to the various information systems before they were implemented.

By May, the Community Tracing Collaborative was reaching 90 percent of people referred to it—a leading performance in the nation. Strong performance was attracting more and more communities of all sizes from across the state to opt in. Whereas in the spring, only several dozen cities and towns were reporting their positive cases to the organization, by September the collaborative was working with 150 municipalities.

Nevertheless, the program stumbled in the late fall. In just a few weeks, the number of positive cases referred grew from several hundred to more than two thousand—each day. With the drop in Covid cases through the summer, we had reduced staff accordingly. Now, there simply was not enough staff to handle the quickly increasing volume.

A course correction was required. In just a month, from November 15 to December 15, more than 1,500 new staffers were hired, doubling the number of the call-center personnel. Further adjustments were made to increase the number of cases and contacts reached every hour, every day, including more staff training, improved support to assist with non-English speakers, and continuing enhancements to the technology systems. By mid-December, the Community Tracing Collaborative was back in good form. By the end of December, the collaborative was regularly connecting with eight thousand to ten thousand people each day, and more than two hundred communities were using its services. Two-thirds of all Massachusetts positive test cases and contacts were being referred to the organization. It was reaching nearly four times as many people in December (120,000) as it had in May (32,000). The collaborative had successfully adjusted in real time, using a constant focus on how.

What to Do and How to Do It

Focusing on how is the engine of the Results Framework. It's a recognition that talented, smart, well-intentioned people alone are not enough, and an acknowledgment that being science-based and data-driven is not sufficient by itself. Follow-through is everything. *How* is about the capacity to perform so that good people guided by the facts can succeed faster, better. Focusing on how is about using strategy and structure to get things done.

Focus on how is the term that wraps together what to do and how to do it. *What* describes policies, programs, and proposals to address the problem defined by the facts. *How* provides the implementation. Together, these two elements move an effort from intent to results.

Both parts of focusing on how are essential. In *what*, policy sets the parameters and goals. A program describes the new services and functions. Laws and budgets provide the enabling language and resources. The outcome is an announcement, a law, a program description, a budget appropriation. This is about what is being recommended. It's about what is going to happen. In effect, it's a charter of activities. It is about intention, direction, and guidance. *What* is powerful because it is an implicit promise to address the problem defined. In the public sector, the emphasis on what to do is so important that, practically speaking, every major agency (state, county, large city) has a staff dedicated to the legislative and budget process.

The next step—*how*—is a fulfillment of the charter. The effort here requires a different kind of attention, skill set, and experience. It's about the operations—the translation from design to delivery. It requires an understanding of how things work. Failing to perform here means disappointment, a promise broken, a problem not resolved or, even worse, exacerbated.

Sometimes the problem and what to do to solve it are straightforward, and the *how* is, too. For example, in March 2020, to address the problem that Covid-19 was threatening to overwhelm the hospital system, we issued a public health emergency order requiring hospitals to postpone any elective procedures. The order was clear and direct, and although it was not simple, the hospitals knew how to make it work.

However, for tough, deeply rooted, and complex problems, attention must not waiver from *how* after the work to define *what* has been done. We believe that *how* is an essential priority requiring top-level attention.

The Affordable Care Act exemplifies a case in which an emphasis on *what* (the legislative fight) and not enough attention to *how* (effective implementation) spelled disaster. After lengthy congressional battles led to its enactment in 2013, the new law offered the promise of a massive expansion of access to health care. But not enough attention had gone toward the operations and IT systems that were to implement this opportunity. Confusion reigned. At first, not only did few individuals gain new health-care coverage, but some lost their existing insurance. Eventually, a crisis team was brought in to focus on delivery. Today, although there are still rough patches in its overall implementation, Obamacare is viewed as a success, providing more than 20 million Americans with health-care coverage.

Too many change efforts fall short in similar ways. It's not just the work involved in creating a new law, or securing additional budget funds, or developing new program features that is needed. The mission is not complete without the attention to implementation and execution that is the ultimate measure of success. In other words, being able to describe the problem and even to make suggestions about what might be needed to address it is one thing. Making it happen—marshaling the people, resources, and know-how to implement the solution—is quite another.

Our attention on how to do it differentiated us from other administrations. A typical call from the executive office to an agency about an issue might be summarized as "fix it *now*!" But we knew it was about how. For us, that meant follow the facts to understand what to do and then launch a full-scale effort focused on how to do it. We believe that such a focus should be elevated in importance to match the public sector's emphasis on policy and programs.

The Art of the Rollout

Tips Tools and Tactics

Implementing a new policy? Releasing a major report? Changing the operation of a program? In the private sector, the element of surprise underlies each business's battle for market share, first-mover position, and new products. But in the public sector, we must work together. No one likes to be surprised, especially those elected officials, partner agencies, and other involved colleagues. And let's not forget customers (residents, families, businesses) that may be impacted.

Remember: change is always tough to execute. Change that is disruptive, or unnecessarily catches people off guard, can provoke a strong reflexive reaction or evoke a defensive crouch. On the other hand, a simple heads-up offers a sense of respect, providing a potential path forward, and preparing the ground for the change. Planning a rollout is a critical part of an initiative's communication efforts. While there are important communication steps along the way, the attention to the rollout is its own specific task.

1. Start by identifying key partners, legislators, and other decision makers, and important constituencies that need to

---

Decision-making: The who, what, when, and where

Set clear project governance. We refer here *not* to governance in the political sense but to governance as in decision-making and accountability. Even when people and resources have been secured, and goals and activities are clear, common trap number one is failing to know. (We have made it a practice to reach out to the House speaker, Senate president, and other members of the legislative leadership in advance of filing major legislation, issuing a significant report, and making a substantial programmatic change.)

2. Develop the details. Assign responsibility for the detailed communication rollout plan: (a) indicate the players to be contacted (legislators, top advocates, key organizations), (b) who will be doing the outreach, and (c) whether the communication is a phone call, email, press release, or emailed documents.

3. Set the timing of the rollout.

4. Write an hourly script of when the specific communication activities are occurring, so that it is clear who is being contacted when. (We have found it useful to begin the script a couple of days before and running throughout the day of the announcement.)

5. Listen to and seek out feedback. Remember, the rollout announcement is the start of this phase of the public announcement. The necessary and important regular communications have just gotten underway.

understand that governance is not about holding positions of authority or org charts, but rather about steering the effort and setting the pace. This step requires clarity about who will make what decisions, who will solicit input from whom, and who will be responsible for implementation. Doubt, confusion, and conflict in decision-making not only mean delay; they are enervating, causing an initiative to falter at the outset or a project with momentum to stall.

While it seems obvious that somebody needs to make decisions and somebody needs to implement them, too many leaders assume that governance is all set, when it is anything but. In complex initiatives with multiple partners, achieving a common understanding about the who, what, when, and where of decision-making is critical.

We recognize that getting governance right does not necessarily mean that the initiative is on track for success. But we do know that without clear governance, the effort will falter, often badly. Further, we know that while strong governance is critical, it must be paired with outstanding leadership and day-to-day management. Because, in the end, a committee or a board can provide direction, but it takes the agency staffers to make it work.

Good ideas, good policies, and good people still require constant monitoring and recalibrating for maximum success. In the fall of 2020, we launched the Eviction Diversion Initiative, a comprehensive effort to provide rental assistance and legal services to help prevent housing evictions resulting from Covid-19 and its economic ripples. In a few weeks, the flow of applications became a flood. Thousands of new rental-assistance applications were being filed each week, and we were not set up to handle the volume.

The initiative's leadership team called a time-out. Our good intention was not matching the reality of what was needed on the ground. This group reviewed how much the work had changed—both the requests for help and the influx of funds had surged. But the governance structure had not kept up. Taking a step back, the team made adjustments—creating some new work streams and dropping others, prescribing precise meeting topics and who needed to be present, and reinforcing clear time frames for getting the work done. This governance reset worked. This clarity in governance provided the focused decision-making and accountability structure needed to make major changes in how the program worked—in a very short time (see chapter 8). Instead of a roadblock, governance became the enabler.

Organizing the work:
Projects, work streams, and teams

In our experience, with the governance structure, including the leadership team, in place, success in getting things done is about how to organize the work. That involves projects, work streams, and a dedicated, mission-oriented team.

We view *projects* as a concrete way to divide what can be an enormous amount of work into units that are meaningful, understandable, and focused on results. A project has a clear beginning and end. Its work plan includes concrete deliverables, allocated resources, metrics for measuring success, and a time frame. Each project has a leader responsible for its successful completion and a team to make it happen.

A *work stream* operates at a higher level, incorporating specific projects. It can include analyzing the facts to understand the problem at hand, a description of activities to address the problem, specific implementation for achieving the desired results, and other related tasks and actions. Work streams give a name and a focus to a set of things that need to be thought about together and integrated with one another. While individual projects make up a significant part of the overall effort, work streams allow for a comprehensive thematic approach that combines the power of project implementation with attention to key ongoing activities like communications, fact research, and policy development.

To organize all these parts and pieces, we use a dedicated, mission-oriented *team* that is focused on coordinating and supporting the entire initiative. This small group is designed to enable success. It helps develop the overall road map and keeps track of the progress of work streams and specific projects. But even more important, it supports leaders and teams to quickly identify and solve problems, jumps in where needed to keep things on track, and foresees the issues ahead. Part traffic control, part schedule master, part handyman, it is critical when much must be done very quickly and well.

Early in our careers, Steve and I were project-based. There were tech projects, operations projects, financial projects, and program-focused projects. A central project-management office monitored efforts, but the approach was one size fits all. Although we had good results, we were looking to do better when starting up in the governor's office.

Combining projects and work streams coordinated by a dedicated team brought together the discipline of projects with the openness and integration of work streams. From the start of the Baker-Polito administration, we employed this practice on major initiatives, especially when the Strategic Ops Team was involved.

Setting the pace: The work-management triangle

In work-management parlance, the triangle sets the parameters for an initiative: it consists of time, scope, and resources. *Time* defines when the project is to be finished. *Scope* describes what is to be achieved. *Resources* are the people, funds, systems, facilities, vendors, and other partners required to deliver the scope. The three are interrelated, and all three have to be kept in mind at all times. For example, it will not work to shorten the time frame and reduce resources while maintaining the scope. Nor will it work to expand the scope while keeping the same time frame and adding no resources. (This might be called magical thinking.)

Of these parameters, we have learned to start with time. Earlier in our careers, we focused on everything that might conceivably be involved in addressing an issue and delivering results. That emphasis on scope could lead to lengthy project timelines with big long-term results but little to show along the way. Especially with tech-related initiatives, we too often saw no significant improvement until the project's end. Worse, a sense of urgency was lacking.

Starting with time flipped the triangle. At the beginning of the Baker-Polito administration, instead of asking what needed to be done and then using scope to determine time and resources, we set targets of a few weeks for the delivery of improvements. That short time frame exploded with urgency, and the effort was laser-focused on the most important things to address. New rounds of projects and actions would follow, building on and learning from what had just been implemented. In this way, the work was broken down from monthslong or multiyear efforts into chunks that provided meaningful improvements over the short term. In project parlance, we were abandoning the traditional "waterfall" approach to embrace an "agile" approach with daily progress reports, speedy adjustments, and rapid results.

As mentioned earlier, a dramatic example was setting a two-week deadline for the Community Tracing Collaborative to make its first calls to Covid-19-positive individuals. To meet the deadline, the team rapidly developed a slim but functional system with improvements to follow. Being able to make and track some calls so quickly was significantly preferable to being unable to make any of those critical connections. What typically would take months to achieve was accomplished in days.

Urgency battles the status quo. Even when the problems to be solved are clear and the concepts to resolve them have been delineated, we must battle against the status quo—the unspoken force that works to keep things as they are. Its power is perilous, especially in bureaucracies. Things happen as they do for specific reasons—history, past practice, workplace rules, even the interpretation of legislative requirements—and the cumulative power of the status quo is energized to maintain itself.

Urgency can be a trigger for change. Urgency can disrupt the status quo, but it must be evident. It communicates that real results must be achieved both quickly and effectively. It creates aggressive deadlines. Every hour, every day, matters. New approaches are adopted. The organization stretches and does things differently. Urgency uses time as a tool.

Assessing progress: Leadership team reviews

Open and honest discussion of an initiative's work streams and projects is a powerful force for getting things done. For us, leadership team reviews are the open-air forum. Organized and supported by the dedicated (aka project-management) team, these review sessions provide a practical, no-drama, just-the-facts assessment of progress and problems. Participants include the leaders of the overall initiative and the key team leaders and subject experts. These meetings go beyond updates. They are critical moments for tracking progress in order to remove roadblocks, deliver needed resources, make changes in scope, identify project interdependencies, resolve problems, and reset deadlines. Although it is always easier to talk about good news, it is critical to highlight what's not working. Over the years, in both the public and the private sectors, we used a straightforward project tracker at our leadership team meetings to enable these sometimes difficult conversations. These reviews provide an opportunity to learn where things stand and then make the adjustments needed to achieve timely, effective results.

We think about tracking status as the project-management version of "If it's not measured, it's not managed." We like to track as much as is practical right from the beginning: work stream progress, project deadlines, staffers hired, budget spent, and key metrics. While narrative comments are always helpful for deeper explanation and context, tracking status is an objective assessment of an initiative's progress. By measuring progress, leadership and the team are in a position to better manage.

We like the simplicity of green-yellow-red for tracking status. Green means the effort is on track and on time. Yellow means that issues have arisen, but it appears that they will be resolved in time to meet the deadline. Red is a call for help. Marking an item red is not easy. It calls attention to issues that cannot be resolved by the project team or the operations team alone. It means that leadership needs to make decisions to get things back on track. But it's a call for resolution, not a condemnation or signal of failure.

We've learned that just as red does not necessarily mean failure, green does not necessarily mean success. Are there any issues of concern? Were deadlines pushed out to make everything green? Are the goals not ambitious enough? Is the environment not open to hearing an objective assessment? These are instances when the team and leadership need to engage in honest reflection and inquiry.

For us, the green-yellow-red tracker shines a light on progress or lack thereof. It allows leadership and the team to focus on the items that need the most immediate attention. While green is always most welcome, the courage and honesty to indicate red are appreciated. We remain wary of shooting the messenger. In fact, leaders have a responsibility to create an environment in which it is safe to use red.

At the beginning of an initiative, these reviews typically occur at least once a day, as was the case with critical efforts early on in the Baker-Polito administration and more recently with the Covid-19 response. However, the frequency should meet the need. In fact,

Checklist to Green

Tips Tools and Tactics

Sometimes projects get the nod to go ahead, but little happens. Leaders are assigned, but not much else. The Checklist to Green helps ensure that initiatives get launched, carried out, refined, and completed. If progress on a project does slip, the checklist functions to get things back on track. Getting to green means that *all* these specific items are developed, understood, and resourced.

The checklist is especially useful when multiple efforts are all being launched simultaneously so that each prong is completely tracked. Here is a ten-point countdown of checklist items:

1. Name the full team needed, including expert and project-management resources (people are policy).

2. Perform solid internal data analysis and gather external information (facts: data evidence).

3. Understand the impact of the problem on customers (facts: points of pain).

4. Define the problem to be solved in a succinct statement with clear results (what to do).

when we were trying to get the Massachusetts Bay Transportation Authority system literally back on track, Steve established check-in meetings as often as four times a day. Once an initiative is well underway and making progress, there may be daily check-ins on specific items, but the leadership team review is needed only once or twice a week.

5. Target changes and new programs to achieve these results (what to do).

6. Ensure clear leadership and governance structure for speedy decision-making (how to do it).

7. Develop the work plan, and use project management to drive implementation (how to do it).

8. Set time frames aggressively—make urgency palpable (how to do it).

9. Conduct timely communication with key constituents and the media (how to do it).

10. Identify performance metrics at the beginning and conduct regular progress reviews by leadership (push for results).

With all checkpoints good to go, the project gets the green light to launch!

The Checklist to Green can be used formally and informally. It can serve as a mental checklist in reviewing projects, or it can be set up as a formatted template with the specific items noted and each item's progress tracked with green, yellow, or red markers.

Planning for Murphy's law

Even with this approach, things sometimes don't work out. Any major initiative worth doing is its own journey into unknown territory. Even with a good plan and a road map, setbacks, disappointments, and detours are bound to occur. While a good plan gives you a good shot at succeeding, we'll take an A+ implementation over an

A+ plan every time. After all, it is the follow-through to the results that has the impact.

For us, this means sweat the details. Clearly describe the change or the new program, but also break down each activity needed to implement it. It's not enough just to get the IT application up and running. You must understand what the key process and information handoffs are and make sure they work. When rolling out a new program, service, or product, you should test, pilot, and practice before going live. Ensure a consistent, honest, and helpful communication internally and with the public. Good communication builds partners and enables trust. And if implementation begins to slip, act quickly to identify and resolve problems and clearly delineate next steps. Good planning is important. Great execution is essential.

Murphy's law is real. If something can wrong, it very likely will. Some things matter more than others. For items that are critical, examine in advance how they might fail—and then plan for prevention or a response. There's truth in the maxim "An ounce of prevention is worth a pound of cure."

If a crisis does occur, address it immediately. Even with very experienced leaders, a strong team, project support, resources, and a good plan, stuff happens. The longer it goes unaddressed or unresolved, the harder it will be to get back on track.

Focusing on how is not a guarantor of success but an enabler. It is not a rigid doctrine but a demonstrated set of practiced and practical principles that achieve results. It is not one and done but instead requires sustained attention and effort—a push—again and again—for results.

4

Push for Results

The winter of 2015 will not soon be forgotten by anyone then living in Massachusetts. It started off relative calmly. However, by late January, we were anxiously tracking the weather forecasts. A major blizzard was on its way. It looked to be a big storm even for Boston, which is accustomed to snow. The leadership at the Massachusetts Emergency Management Agency was recommending that a state of emergency be declared. On January 26, the blizzard began. It was the sixth-biggest snowstorm on record to hit Boston, dropping more than two feet of snow in much of the state. That afternoon, after only eighteen days as governor, I announced a state of emergency. State offices would be shuttered, schools would be closed, the National Guard would be positioned in key areas to help, and a travel ban would take effect at midnight. The Massachusetts Bay Transportation Authority (MBTA), metro Boston's public transit system, made an unusual announcement: Service would stop. No buses, no streetcars, no commuter trains, no nothing.

Five days later, on February 2, another sixteen inches of snow fell. I called another snow emergency. Schools and businesses were closed again. Then, for the third time in less than two weeks, a storm dumped nearly two feet of snow. It was our eighth-biggest storm on record.

In thirty days, from January 24 to February 22, a record ninety-four inches of snow fell. To put this in perspective, the average annual snowfall in Boston was just over forty-three inches. By March 15, 108 inches—*nine feet*—of snow had fallen at Boston's Logan Airport. That year we used the figure of a Boston Celtics player with his outstretched arm just short of the rim to measure the snow. Even worse, temperatures stayed unusually cold. Boston recorded twenty-eight consecutive days with lows of twenty degrees or below, breaking the record set in 1881. We called it Snowmageddon.

Of all the issues we had to face with this weather challenge, it was the unexpected failure of the MBTA, popularly known as the T, that caused the most distress and disruption to Boston and the surrounding communities of eastern Massachusetts. The MBTA normally provided more than 1.2 million rides a day, making connections to work, school, medical appointments, shopping, restaurants, and the other stuff of life.

When the MBTA stopped, we all stopped. It was a domino effect of enormous proportions. More than one of every three people who worked in metro Boston took the MBTA to get to work. And there was little alternative. The streets were barely passable for traffic, and huge piles of snow filled any possible parking space. The Massachusetts economy lost billions of dollars in the span of a few weeks. From one perspective, Massachusetts, the vaunted twenty-first-century tech hub, had come up against the age-old power of Mother Nature—and Mother Nature had won. But when we looked under the hood—or in this case, the snow cover—we found a different story. Decades of underinvestment in and under-attention to the MBTA had come home to roost.

After the third storm shut down service for the second time within just a few days, the MBTA's general manager, Beverly Scott, held a press conference. For staid old Boston, the media event was a fiery affair. The *Boston Globe* reported: "During her passionate, defiant, and at times rambling news conference on Tuesday, Scott pointed out that there was little anyone could do to make trains that are practically antiques run on snowpacked rails and frozen switches."[1]

Two days later, although she had just received the unanimous support of the Massachusetts Board of Transportation, Scott took everyone by surprise. She announced her resignation, to take effect two months later.

In the meantime, we had scheduled a meeting with her. I held my initial meeting with Beverly at the MBTA's headquarters, rather than ask her to come to me in the governor's office. No public announcement. No media. I wanted an opportunity to have a frank discussion of the situation and to understand what the plans were for going forward.

When Steve and I arrived, Bev and her team were positioned around a long, U-shaped table in a conference room with large windows overlooking downtown Boston. More than twenty people, including a few governor's office staffers, sat at attention. The general manager made her introductory remarks, and I followed. The other people around the table introduced themselves. The atmosphere was tense and awkward.

After a brief status update from Beverly, I asked everyone at the table who wished to speak to do so. I wanted to learn what was happening directly and to hear the various perspectives. After a few MBTA staffers had spoken, it became clear to everyone in the room that the organization's standard operating procedures were inadequate and no practical plans for recovery had been made.

I was conducting an impromptu round-the-table discussion not only to encourage the participants to speak, but also to provide an in-person message that this would be a new approach to problem-solving. No finger-pointing. No raised voices. Beverly readily accepted my offer of assistance.

We began with "people are policy." At that meeting, Beverly tapped her deputy general manager to lead the recovery effort, and I indicated that Steve would lead the governor's office support: help from the Strategic Operations and Communications staff and access to other state resources, from procurement to the National Guard.

The MBTA had not previously considered those resources. It was clear to us that some staffers at the MBTA had a wealth of information but not the requisite experience to confront this emergency. The agency had always done things on its own, and it had more or less worked out. Now it was overwhelmed, and we wanted to bring the full support of state government to help. Two state agencies gave us access to their snow-removal contractors and equipment. The state purchasing agent and the emergency services office offered access to supplies and contractors for road salt and sand. These tangible additions to the recovery effort also demonstrated new thinking, which would be needed to address the ongoing emergency.

With Steve and the governor's Strategic Ops staff facilitating, the team took a follow-the-facts approach to gather data and catalog points of pain. It reviewed every mile of track, every station, every locomotive, every maintenance facility, every major track switch, and all snow-removal equipment to determine their functional status. It acted as quickly, deliberately, and thoroughly as possible in a very short time. We soon established a baseline assessment of what was working and what was literally buried beneath the snow.

What to do quickly emerged from the follow-the-facts analysis. Next it was to focus on how. We had three main problems:

1. **Move the snow!** Miles and miles of tracks had to be cleared. Past practice had called for the MBTA's trains themselves to be a primary means of removing snow from the tracks. That

may have worked with smaller amounts of snow, but this amount proved overpowering. Trains had blown up their motors and shut down. Furthermore, there was no plan for moving so much snow out of maintenance yards. Trains could not get in and out of the maintenance sheds for critical repairs. And even where the trains were running, mountains of snow blocked passengers from getting to stations and bus stops.

2. **Fix the engines!** Never in anyone's experience had so many subway cars and trains been shut down because of equipment failure. The snow had blown up the traction motors in much of the core subway system's fleet and the inventory of replacement motors had quickly been wiped out in the first storm. Further, a host of equipment and maintenance problems knocked out the engines of the commuter rail system. "For want of a nail, the kingdom was lost" seemed true for the MBTA. Without a functioning MBTA, metro Boston stopped. Fixing the traction motors and train engines became the highest priority among the equipment issues that plagued the aging fleet.

3. **Communicate!** From schools to employers to medical facilities, everyone needed to know what was happening at the MBTA and what service would be provided when. The agency wasn't set up for the kind of ongoing, proactive, broad communication that we were all so hungry for.

Teams were established to propose how to attack those three *what to dos*. An intense project-management approach drove the effort to develop specific recovery actions and track progress. Leadership meetings were held as often as four times a day, from as early as 7 a.m. to focus on the morning commute to as late as 8 p.m. to review

Communication Keys

Tips Tools and Tactics

While communication is important in the private sector, it is essential in the public sector. A full-on communications plan is a requirement for successful initiatives. In the public sector, with so many involved stakeholders, timely, accurate, and helpful communications can mean the difference between an unnecessary stumble or solid progress. You can have a strong team, know the facts, create good program options, and develop a strong implementation plan, but if there's not also a good communication plan, the initiative has an Achilles' heel.

Larger agencies and organizations may have media teams, PR consultants, or a team member charged with communication. Your organization may not be able to allocate a full-time communications person, but there must be a clear communications plan and the people to execute. Find ways to go through these steps:

1. Involve those responsible for communications in leadership and team meetings. This will ground the communications folks in the important aspects of the project, and they, in turn, will help raise key questions that otherwise may not have been considered.

the day and prepare for the following morning. Media updates were scheduled twice a day, more if needed.

Together, the governor's office and the MBTA staff developed green-yellow-red tracking charts for each performance metric to make issues and progress vivid: line by line (tracks cleared of snow?

2. Develop a communications plan for the whole project and discreet sub-plans for each phase. In chapter 3, we discuss the communications involved with the initiative's public rollout. This is only one piece of the communications plan. In fact, the communications plan—the various audiences, the important messages, and the means to communicate— should be developed right from the project start and adjusted as the initiative progresses. Each phase of the project (development, rollout, implementation, and then ongoing operations) involves different people and partners.

3. Secure the specific people and resources needed to develop and execute the plan. Communications will involve many people, including team leaders, program staff, and budget analysts to help with writing, review, and fact-checking.

4. Communication involves a lot more than a CEO or project leader sending an email. Good communication is a two-way street. It requires inspired listening. It requires a sincere interest in feedback. Listening to various audiences is part of the feedback loop that is critical to measuring results and making course corrections.

cracked rails caused by the deep freeze repaired?), train by train (blown engines replaced? other needed parts installed?), station by station (doorways cleared of snow and accessible to passengers?), passenger by passenger (communications clear on schedule changes and expectations?).

That intense project management allowed the leadership team to laser-focus on a defined set of key tasks, learn what had been accomplished, and be notified of problems. Speedy problem identification and same-time decision-making was followed by quick implementation.

Several times a day at our leadership review meetings, performance metrics steadily improved. In the end, it took about half the time originally estimated to get MBTA subway and bus services back to fully functioning. And it took only about one month more to get full service back on the commuter rail—weeks ahead of the original estimate.

That success set an important example for initiatives to follow.

Lessons from the Private Sector

From the beginning of the Baker-Polito administration, we brought a focus on results. *Push for results* means to determine not only whether the outcomes match the goals of the initiative—to fix a problem, to improve a program, to offer a new service—but are the specific interventions actually working. We wanted to take what we had learned in the private sector about measuring performance and integrate it in how public services were delivered. In the private sector, metrics are de rigueur: the survival of an organization depends on them. Not so, usually, in the public sector, where the focus is more often on the program narrative, legislation, and funding. Performance might be an afterthought or became important only when something failed. We wanted performance to be as important as the enabling intent, laws, and budgets.

Our experience at Harvard Pilgrim Health Care drove home the value of measurable results. With the potential failure of the business looming, it became crystal clear that we needed to understand where progress had been made and how to continue and accelerate it. When performance was faltering, we needed to know what changes to make.

Three levels of performance metrics would matter. First, what are the top-line results? Second, what's happening with key services, programs, and products? Third, what does all this mean at the individual-transaction level? At Harvard Pilgrim, the top-level review meant profit and loss and the total number of members. Was the budget net positive or negative? Was the number of customers increasing or decreasing? If so, how fast? The second-level review was an analysis of the costs and outcomes of specific products. Were some health insurance options better at meeting customer needs than others? Were specific program and operations expenses comparable with those of our peers? The third level involved a deeper dive. What were the experiences of individuals dealing with our member services, employers trying to understand health-care costs and level of services, or health-care providers seeking timely reimbursement? Here we addressed the human stories—the points of pain. Getting the results right would literally make or break Harvard Pilgrim.

This experience showed us what measuring results could mean for the public sector. In the public sector, although a review of top-line results was common when budgets were evaluated, and might drive some specific second-level review, it was the next level, the focus on individual experiences, that often illuminated how things worked. We could measure how long it would take to answer the phone and resolve an issue in member services. We could measure costs to an employer for an employee's health care. And we could measure timely reimbursement to providers for their services.

Taken together, individual experiences would build the total organizational performance. Removing a point of pain means not only that a problem has been solved but also that the organization's performance is improving.

Align metrics to meet goals

Ultimately, Harvard Pilgrim had performance metrics for all three levels, which we reviewed in the weekly leadership meetings. Decisions and adjustments were made quickly. Subsequent performance metrics were evaluated. More adjustments were implemented as necessary. In retrospect, we were battle-tested for what was to come in the public sector.

As governor of Massachusetts, I wanted to make this discipline of measuring results core to the way my administration worked. I wanted to bring this private-sector focus on outcomes to public-sector priorities. Not the private sector's measures of profit, margins, or growth. They aren't measures of success in the public sector—and shouldn't be. But we did want to take full account of how well services are performed as individual transactions and as a whole, using, for example, measures such as *timeliness*: how long it took to conduct a transaction at the Registry of Motor Vehicles or to complete an application to receive unemployment; *access*: to health care, transportation, or childcare; *customer service* at our agencies' call centers: how long wait times were, and what percentage of calls were abandoned or never answered; and *financial efficiency*: In a budget-constrained world, were funds being maximized to deliver more services of high quality?

This comprehensive push for results was the culmination of meeting our biggest goals. For Harvard Pilgrim Health Care, this meant not just getting out of financial trouble, but becoming one of the top-performing health insurance providers in the nation. For the MBTA, while getting back to a semblance of operations was a must, the overriding goal was a reliable, efficient public transit service. In each of these examples (and others throughout the book), setting the big goal provided the context and definition of success. The intense focus on performance metrics at all three levels allows a full accounting of progress.

Distrust averages

We believe that managing with metrics is not just helpful but essential. But managing with bad metrics or the wrong metrics is as bad as managing without any metrics at all. Weak data distorts the conclusions. Worse, it can result in actions that don't address the right issues. That's one reason we hate averages.

When a presentation starts with "On average, we have found . . . ," our eyebrows furl. Why? Because averages hide what's actually going on at the individual level. They can mask the extremes and make things seem OK. Here's a simple example: if you have a bunch of ninety-degree days and an equal bunch of forty-degree days, the average is a very comfortable sixty-five degrees. Really?

In too many instances, averages don't tell the true story. When we started looking at on-time performance at the MBTA, the averages presented mirrored that temperature example. A traveler during non-peak commuting hours experienced relatively timely service. But when trains were the busiest and most crowded—during morning and afternoon rush hours—on-time performance deteriorated. Yet the average didn't look too bad.

The same was true at the Registry of Motor Vehicles. In 2015, the time it took to serve a customer averaged more than an hour. Not terrible for something that was known for horrendous delays. But why did this agency receive so many complaints from so many people about the wait? The average masked the fact that people at less-busy locations had relatively short waits, while those who might have less flexibility and had to go at busy times to busy locations might be there a couple of hours or more.

The processing of rental-assistance applications was similarly vexing. In January 2021, it averaged six to ten weeks, depending on the local agency handling the application. Too long, but manageable. Yet this average concealed the fact that hundreds of applications dated back to the previous summer.

In each of these cases, it wasn't until the team broke down the actual experience of the individual customer that we understood what was going on. Overall, it was a lesson in how looking at the right metrics helps drive the actions that improve the customer experience.

Discuss results in the open

The legendary UCLA basketball coach John Wooden once said, "Never mistake activity for achievement." For our work, it's not about being busy with meetings, emails, phone calls, and Zoom conferences—all of which are necessary. It's about what actions and solutions are discussed in those communications and which ones make a difference. While we recognize that inputs matter and process is important, especially in the public sector, we use metrics to measure the results.

Tracking those figures and collecting data are basic, but they're not enough. That data has to be evaluated regularly and then acted on quickly. To ensure that this happens, a discussion of performance metrics needs to be a standard agenda item in leadership review meetings.

The significance of this simple but important concept—discussing metrics in a forum that matters—came from our time at Harvard Pilgrim. There, weekly leadership committee meetings had a regular agenda item for presenting, dissecting, and discussing performance metrics. The message was clear. If these metrics are important to the CEO, the COO, the CFO, and all the other members of the C-suite, they should be important to everyone in the organization. In these review sessions, successes, missed targets, unusual events, strong performances, and weak results were shared. As the implementation continued, new metrics emerged, and some were dropped or reviewed on a less-frequent basis.

For the metrics review to be as valuable as possible to the organization, and invigorating rather than enervating for the participants, we had to create an environment where questions were accepted and discussion was safe. Looking at a target and the related increases or decreases in numbers, percentage changes, trends, and other graphics, and discussing what they mean, why, and what can be done, allows for unprejudiced dialogue. Attention moves from the messenger to the message—the facts and context of the presentation. By being clear that anyone could introduce a question, and trying to model helpful ways to ask one, our leadership team cultivated an environment in which it was OK to observe that something wasn't working out, to propose an alternative interpretation, or to recommend a specific intervention without fear of repercussion. In those meetings, we supported honesty about the facts and curiosity as to the circumstances, and we positively reinforced courageously raising the uncomfortable. It was an effort to create a learning environment.

A key goal of those discussions was to take the lessons learned back to the appropriate points in the process. Do the metric results indicate that the initiative needs more people with more experience, a different policy or program intervention, or an adjustment to the approach? Then make the adjustments, fast, and repeat the process to meet performance targets.

Asking a Question

Tips Tools and Tactics

We all learn through inquiry. Yet in organizations of any size, hierarchies influence whether asking or receiving questions is comfortable. A direct question from a hard-charging CEO to a team member can be intimidating. A team member raising a point in a room with a bunch of executives can be perceived as leaping over boundaries, or even impertinent.

But a meeting without robust discussion is a lecture, a one-way presentation. Some of the best insights bubble up from below. And for progress review meetings meant to solve problems, questions are essential to understanding current status, shedding light on thorny issues, and conceiving of imaginative actions.

To make sure participants feel comfortable asking questions when many levels of an organization are in the same meeting, try these steps:

Relentless, incremental progress—not one and done. *Push for results* acts as a rudder for the effort.

Measure. Evaluate. Adjust. Repeat.

Like everything else related to getting things done, the review of metrics and results that we've practiced since the beginning of the Baker-Polito administration achieved its greatest significance with

1. As a presentation ends, all eyes go to the leader or meeting facilitator. Set the right tone. Beginning with a positive comment and/or a sincere "thank you" is a good step.

2. When asking a question or making a point, be respectful in language and manner. Express good intent and not defensiveness, a point of attack, or a counterattack. Listen to the response and follow up as appropriate.

3. Be sure to ask if others have questions. Everyone is in the room for a reason. It's especially important to make sure that those with expertise or an important opinion speak up, so that the full group can consider their questions and comments.

4. Before closing the discussion, ask if there are any other key points to be raised or options to consider.

5. Recap decisions needed and identify next steps before the meeting adjourns. Results of the discussion will drive the momentum coming out of the meeting.

Covid-19. Because understanding the metrics was so important, setting up a performance dashboard was one of the very first priorities of the Covid-19 Response Command Center. Soon the whole state and the nation were following metrics on a daily basis in an unprecedented way. Number of individuals tested for Covid-19. Percentage of positive test results. Number of patients hospitalized and in the ICU. Number of deaths—each day.

Under Secretary Sudder's leadership, the metrics review was the first order of business at Command Center meetings with the lieutenant governor and me. Marylou and her team provided graphics detailing key metrics statewide: number of tests, positive cases, positivity rate, Covid-19-related fatalities, patients hospitalized, contacts reached. The report broke out those numbers by age, gender, race, and town. As time went on, more-detailed information was shared regarding each hospital, nursing home or long-term care facility, schools K–12, and colleges and universities. Most of these metrics became part of the daily and weekly public data displays that informed the public on the state of the virus and our efforts to mitigate its impacts.

The review began with statewide trends and then dove into the details. These metrics reports were not static. While common definitions and measurement were critical, the metrics were adapted as needed to provide a picture of the ever-changing epidemiology of the pandemic.

Marylou was a master of the "So what?" Data is always helpful, but understanding the "So what?" is paramount. It transforms data into useful information. At each Command Center session, this review of the metrics helped guide Karyn and me in determining next steps and what adjustments to make in policy and approach.

As 2020 ended, vaccination metrics were added. The federal government controlled vaccine distribution. Each state learned only several days in advance how many doses it would get, and the number received was frighteningly small compared with the demand and the need. The process was bumpy and frustrating. We clearly did not have enough vaccine supply to meet demand, and the online appointment system was overwhelmed when it rolled out. In February 2021, in what was supposed to be a longed-for moment of relief, I said to the media, "My hair was on fire." We had to do better. Measure, evaluate, adjust—quickly—and repeat was the mantra. Within two weeks, the appointment system had improved. By mid-March, Massachusetts

Working with the Media

Tips Tools and Tactics

As a society, we place high value on a free and robust press in recognition of its role in a functioning democracy. Even so, most politicians and many leaders have a love-hate relationship with a media corps that often seems disinterested in success and ready to pounce on mistakes *or* pick up on points of disagreement. But in the public sector, we are correctly and perpetually judged by our words, our actions, and our presence, all of which the media amplifies.

As a group, reporters are smart, inquisitive, and resourceful. They investigate, ask questions, and link concepts, all to tell a story to their audience. The give-and-take is always challenging, and sometimes uncomfortable. But the media makes us better at what we do. So, it behooves the public-sector leader to figure out how to embrace the give-and-take.

Here are some pointers (learned the hard way):

- **Make time to be available.** You are both the messenger and the message. Reporters are proxies for the public that cannot be there. When they ask questions, they are doing their jobs. Answer them. Also, repeat important messages and then repeat them again and again ("Wear a Mask!" "Vaccines Saves Lives!").

- **Make time to prepare.** Block the time in your schedule for this work. Review and know the facts of topics you will be discussing. Practice the delivery of your message. Role-play

(continued)

the obvious questions. If you are giving formal remarks, write down what you are going to say. If your statements are prepared by staff, review and be comfortable with word choice and phrasing.

- **Determine the forum.** Work with your team and communications leads to decide when you will speak to reporters, and whether you do best in formal or informal settings. Be deliberate in choosing to use a press release, text, or other posting, and be cognizant of how these messages will be received and understood.

- **Know the rules.** If you like talking to reporters on the phone or trading texts, figure out a way to have a record of the exchange. Take some time to learn the attribution basics, beyond "on the record" and "off the record," which are often misunderstood categories.

- **Get to know the reporters covering you.** Members of the media are people with lives, interests, families, and histories. They also have to answer to editors and publishers. And they don't write headlines. Pay attention to the ones you can trust the most to get a story right and create a virtuous circle. Be fair in distributing your attention.

was the top performer among large states, and a few weeks later, we became the top performer among all states.

At that time, the *Boston Globe* reported on our vaccine rollout: "Call it folding to public pressure or just responsive government, Governor Charlie Baker's vaccine rollout has been full of twists and turns, some of them 180-degrees," the article said. "[T]he governor emphasized he is receptive to feedback. 'I've said this for six years, that if we get input from others that says, If you could do this, this would be better, we try to do that,' Baker said."[2]

Our approach includes listening to input and learning from our actions. We measure results, evaluate what changes need to be made, make adjustments, and keep repeating the metrics review process.

Although each of the preceding chapters can stand on its own, the full success of the Results Framework comes when the individual components are brought together. Then you have a comprehensive approach that produces substantive positive change. In part 2, we will tell four stories in detail, as each addresses a critical set of issues and demonstrates the impact of the Results Framework. We've chosen these particular Massachusetts stories—about health care, transportation, children and families, and Covid-19—because we believe that they will resonate deeply with anyone who delivers, or depends, on public service, anywhere around the country or even around the world.

PART TWO

Applying the Results Framework

How to Use the Four Steps to Solve Big, Gnarly Problems

5

From Worst to First

Health Care

Governor Baker Forces Resignation of 4 Health Connector Board Members," read the headline on the website of the local NPR affiliate.[1] We weren't the only ones who thought it was a striking move, especially given that the administration was only six weeks old.

The Massachusetts Health Connector's operational problems had been a top media story for more than a year leading up to the start of my term. But it wasn't always so. The Connector had been established in 2006 under then-Governor Mitt Romney as part of a comprehensive health-care-reform effort. The Romney team had developed this innovative mechanism as a state-sponsored exchange where people could buy commercial health insurance that was more affordable than what they could obtain on their own. It allowed lower-income individuals to get insurance at subsidized rates with lower premiums and co-pays. The Connector offered a simple and elegant approach to one of the most frustrating problems in health care—access to affordable coverage. After several years of success, it had been a model for the federal Affordable Care Act that was signed into law by President Barack Obama in 2010.

However, adapting the state program to meet new federal requirements would involve significant changes in technology and process before the fall 2013 open enrollment, which was when existing and potential customers could select a health plan for the following year. Previous open enrollments had proceeded without significant hitches. But by the beginning of 2014, it was clear this one was a disaster. The *New York Times* reported that, according to its own analysis, the state "was last in the nation in meeting enrollment goals, signing up only 5,428 applicants in private plans."[2]

Some were blaming management; some were pointing fingers at the company that had implemented the technology. A *Vox* article summed it up: "Massachusetts officials tried to pull off an ambitious launch—and failed badly."[3] Throughout 2014, the troubles at the Connector made not only for regular media headlines, but also for a rash of questions posed on the campaign trail.

On November 15, one week after the 2014 election, Governor Deval Patrick's administration began the next open enrollment, which was scheduled to run through February 15, 2015. I took office on January 8 with enrollment well underway. Would all the time and money spent in the months leading up to this new enrollment period lead to a smooth process or a rerun of the previous year's painful experience? Within days of taking office, we learned the answer.

As part of our early-morning routine, after Steve and I had our usual one-to-one call, he convened key members of the governor's office staff. This daily conference call allowed us to put out critical information so that everyone could begin the day on the same page. From 7:45 to 8:00 a.m., we had rapid-fire updates on the media, the legislature, events in Washington, and concerns raised through constituent services. On these calls we first learned that frustration with the Connector continued to build. Perhaps it was because of my experience as the CEO of Harvard Pilgrim Health Care that I so deeply understood the consequences for individuals and families of not knowing whether they had health-care coverage.

People contact the governor's office for all kinds of reasons. Under our administration, those requesting a meeting or an event with the governor would be directed to scheduling. People looking for a job with the new administration were referred to HR. All others were referred to constituent services. Opinions on legislation, complaints about a state service, or simple requests for information were noted there and sent to the appropriate agency for a response. As part of the daily staff call, constituent services reported on the types and numbers of incoming emails, letters, and phone calls. Typically, the incoming messages represented a wide variety of topics. Exceptions occurred for certain legislative items, when various organizations pushed supporters to contact the governor. But even in those cases, messages from the public rarely exceeded double digits for a few days.

In these first few weeks of the Baker-Polito Administration, complaints about the Health Connector lit up the phone lines. This wasn't an organized effort to pass legislation or secure more funding for something. These were individuals who were frustrated, worried, and angry because they couldn't get the answers they needed about their health-care coverage. They had called the Connector without success. Could they go to surgery as planned? Could they take their children to the doctor? Had the payment been received? Did they have health-care coverage? The number of calls grew every day.

It became apparent that for the second year in a row, the Health Connector's open enrollment had flopped. We would soon learn that thousands of individuals and families were affected. Worse, the Connector's staff apparently couldn't handle all the phone calls and didn't have answers for the ones they could handle. As the call volume increased, we discussed how to fix the problems. Just before I took office, its executive director had resigned.

Putting the People in Place

In discussions about candidates for executive director of the Connector, Louis Gutierrez was at the top of the list. Both Steve and I had worked with Louis in state government and at Harvard Pilgrim Health Care. Among other things, we knew Louis was a proven collaborator. He was also a brilliant information-systems technologist who understood how the convergence of operations and technology made things work. Louis recognized that although it can offer huge leaps in getting things done, technology alone is almost never the answer. In fact, technology change without a holistic approach to customer impact and the changes required in operations is too often a path to disaster. Two consecutive open-enrollment failures painfully illustrated a technology rollout without clarity on the operational impact.

While strong executive leadership was essential to addressing these problems, so was governance, by which we mean decision-making and accountability. The Connector's governing board had eleven members, including four gubernatorial appointees, three appointees of the attorney general, and four others whose seats were determined by their positions in state government. Appointees served staggered terms. Unless some action was taken, another year—and another open enrollment—would have passed before I could name a majority of the board.

With Louis as the Connector's new executive director, we had a shot. But how could we run an effective turnaround when the board itself might be operating at cross-purposes, unwilling to make the necessary changes? I had experienced a similar situation firsthand at Harvard Pilgrim Health Care. When I arrived as CEO, the board that had brought the organization to the brink of bankruptcy was unable to address the dire situation at hand. A new board helped lead the organization to become the number one health plan in the nation.

Changing the board

Part of taking responsibility for fixing the Connector's problems was putting our team on the field. I wanted to be sure that everyone involved was aligned on getting this situation fixed fast. After conferring with Lieutenant Governor Karyn Polito, I decided to ask the four current gubernatorial appointees to resign.

I certainly hadn't won the 2014 election by a landslide. But if I had a mandate, it was to fix what was broken in state government. For two years, the Health Connector had been a poster child for what wasn't working. Much was at stake. A broken Connector threatened the health insurance coverage of more than 200,000 people. And because the Connector and our Medicaid program shared parts of a technology platform, failure at the Connector disrupted Medicaid, with considerable implications for the state budget and federal financial support.

The Health Connector team that was in place—the board, management, and the key consultants—just hadn't done their jobs. Replacing some board members now would ensure that the Connector's leadership and management were aligned for the tough work ahead. Alignment was not about political ideology. It was about focusing on practical efforts to provide this public service. We needed to know that Louis's proposals to the board would be reviewed on their merits, not in the shadow of some lingering political doubt. The significant changes needed in IT and business operations would take time—often months, if not years. With the next open enrollment only nine months away, we could not afford to wait.

I directed Steve to reach out to the four gubernatorial appointees. I knew it was unusual to ask them to resign. And there was no guarantee that they would agree. By statute, and for their own personal and professional reasons, they were entitled to remain in their positions. Although each one was surprised by the call, they all respected the request. I admired them for that. They stepped aside without fanfare or acrimony. Thankfully, everyone was looking to turn the page.

In addition to naming new members to the board, we had to make another important change. Louis Gutierrez articulated it best. "The biggest system failures I have witnessed had less to do with technology than with project governance," he said. He argued that the most crucial change needed would be transferring the board chairmanship from the secretary of administration and finance to the secretary of health and human services. Louis made this suggestion because he had witnessed antipathy between established Medicaid organizations and new exchange entities in several other states. Institutionally, the status quo invariably resulted in behaviors by established leaders and entrenched staffers that undermined the new entities. It was essential that not happen here. Having the health and human services secretary chair the Connector board would allow for "common parentage" and responsibility for both the Connector and Medicaid.

Building the team

In any organization, a working partnership between it and the CEO is vital. It is especially vital when the organization is in crisis. In Louis, the Connector had a leader with knowledge, experience, and know-how in health care from both the private and the public sectors. To succeed, he would need partners on his management team to help drive change.

A critical piece of building the Connector leadership team would be securing a chief operating officer with extensive experience in health-care operations. Ideally, someone who had been through a successful turnaround. Talent attracts talent. On March 12, Louis announced that Vicki Coates would be the COO, a new role and the clear number two in the organization. Patricia Wada was tapped to be the special assistant for project delivery. We had worked with Vicki at Harvard Pilgrim Health Care and with Patricia on some of the most complicated technology projects in the Commonwealth. In Vicki, the Connector had a straightforward, detail-oriented operations professional. Patricia brought deep practical experience in managing complex public IT projects. Altogether, Louis, Vicki, and Patricia provided the tangible people-are-policy leadership reset to tackle the work ahead.

Louis made further changes, and some staffers decided to leave as a result. But he believed that the existing staff included lots of underused talent that the new leaders would be able to tap. The current employees certainly knew the problems. Louis thought that given the opportunity and support, they would welcome a chance to be part of the fix-it team. Steve and some staffers from the Strategic Operations Team joined the effort. Attempts to fix the Connector in the previous year had fallen far short. Now, under my administration, we would have a new approach and all hands on deck.

Adding consultants

Whether public or private, health insurance entities rely on various third parties—consultants—for critical tasks. For the Connector, they provided member services, eligibility determination, and a host of financial transactions, including collecting monthly premiums and making payments to providers. In other words, the services of the consultants *were* the services of the Connector.

Each one of these services was complex, with its own IT systems and business rules. Further adding to the complexity was the coordination required for handoffs of information between the various systems platforms, because they were interdependent.

For example, a member's monthly payment was calculated in one system, and the receipt of payment was recorded in another. The data exchange between the two operations had to be seamless to provide proof of insurance coverage. When it wasn't, the member would be told by the health-care provider that insurance did not cover the claim. And if a member called to ask why, the call center was not adequately linked with these other systems to provide an accurate response.

As at other health insurance providers, service delivery at the Connector depended on a web of software, hardware, and data exchanges to bring all the details of people, paper, and protocols together. When it works, it's a symphony. When it doesn't, problems pile on problems. In early 2015, if any music was coming from the Massachusetts Health Connector, it was a screech. For two years, the Connector had been a disaster with real consequences for individuals and for the state's health-care budget. If its performance was to improve, the performance of the consultants needed to improve.

Louis had much experience working with consultants. He had also been on the other side as a vendor consultant working on health-care IT implementations. He understood that the success of the Connector depended on its IT infrastructure and service operations. He also understood how central the consultants were to making them work. With Louis now leading, and Vicki and Patricia lending experienced support in health-care operations and IT, the Connector had a top-level team to manage the staff and consultants as they addressed the problems challenging nearly every part of the operation.

Failure at the Call Center

On February 15, 2015, when the annual Health Connector open enrollment ended, it appeared that the Connector had not just a technology problem but a service-operations failure as well. Callers abandoned up to 40 percent of calls.

These customer experiences kicked into gear this initiative's follow the facts, the second step in the Results Framework. The team at the Connector compiled detailed lists of customers' calls—the points of pain—and began to tackle the problems. At the same time, Vicki led a review of all aspects of the member services, financial, and data-exchange operations. The team gathered data and looked at performance metrics, and, in our one-to-one morning calls, Steve gave me updates and we discussed possible next steps.

After several weeks of multiple daily meetings, we had a basis for the third stage in the Results Framework: focus on how. Louis framed the immediate *what to do* as responding to and resolving customers' issues. That meant concentrating on the pain points and stabilizing the system and operations at a basic, reliable level of service. As COO, Vicki drove those operational fixes. The specifics included an overhaul of the call center, a rapid working down the customer-issues list, tackling mistakes and updates to member account information, reinstating member eligibility, ensuring data accuracy for the Connector's health plans, and fixing payment and credit balance errors. Patricia led a simultaneous effort to prepare for the upcoming fall open enrollment.

Working with Consultants

Tips Tools and Tactics

Sometimes consultants bring expertise that the organization lacks and needs quickly. Sometimes consultants bring the resources for a new service or expanded program. Sometimes, consultants bring objective evaluation and fresh concepts for going forward.

When you think you need the help of a consultant, take the time to really understand what the need is and who most appropriately matches it. As these are big and often expensive decisions, here are some tips:

- When engaging a consultant, make it a priority to develop the scope for the work proposed, which provides clarity on the problem to solve, the work to perform, the method for doing it, the outcomes desired, and the time frame.

- As the work is a joint effort of the agency and the consultant, note the roles and resources of the agency in support of but distinct from the consultant.

- Ask for top talent, the A team. Get a commitment on how much time the consultant's leadership will personally devote to this work. As the work proceeds, if someone on the consultant team is not performing as expected, ask to have the person removed and replaced as soon as possible. This is part of your management responsibility.

- Assign top-level experienced individuals from your team to manage any consultants. You have asked for the A team. Give them your A team.

- Don't be passive. Don't expect consultants to step in and take the lead. This is your agency. This is your consultant. This is your job.

- Managing a consultant contract is not the same as managing staff. It requires constant attention to get two distinct organizations to work together. Your agency has its goals, lines of authority, performance evaluation, and procedures. The consultant entity is a separate organization with its own ways of doing business. It takes concerted, continual management to avoid working at cross-purposes and to ensure alignment.

- Hold regular check-ins to assess together what's working and to quickly address what's not. However, meetings and discussion are the beginning, not the end. Write down all agreements so that you and the consultant have a clear understanding of performance.

- Push hard. In the public sector especially, it is important to get to meaningful results as quickly and efficiently as possible. It's the taxpayers' dollars, and your responsibility is to use these consultant resources wisely.

All told, it was a mess. But the Connector team was beginning to get a handle on the scope and size of the issues, and it was developing a plan to move ahead.

Goal: Successful Open Enrollment

Louis knew that stabilizing Connector services and implementing a successful open enrollment had to be a whole-team effort. That meant recognizing a different way of working for all the key participants, from senior-level Connector management to the major consultancies involved.

The foundation of *how to do it* would be a strong project-management approach. Louis and Vicki had been key players in the Harvard Pilgrim Health Care turnaround and had seen the success that active project management could deliver. They realized the importance of breaking down larger work streams into specific projects and then further into tasks. They were practiced in the belief that you manage what you measure and had learned the importance of making adjustments according to actual results. They welcomed the support of the governor's team. At the Connector, project management would give each project a dedicated leader and team with clear task deadlines and accountability. Connector leadership and all other key participants and decision makers, including consultants, would attend regular project reviews to assess the issues and the progress and to engage in problem-solving discussions.

On April 2, 2015, sixty-plus staffers and key consultant team members gathered in a large conference room at the Connector's offices. It was standing room only. For Louis and the team, this day marked the launch of the Connector's turnaround.

At this ninety-minute kickoff meeting, after brief introductions, Louis outlined the "45-Day Plan for Operations Assessment and

What Our Members Are Feeling

"My husband was turned away from his appointment this month because he thought we had coverage and we don't but should have as we paid and were promised! I have inhalers that [are] too costly for me to pay out of pocket and an appointment with my doctor on April 2nd yet last I heard I am not enrolled! Beyond frustrated as this is illegal and no one seems to care enough that hundreds of families in Mass are experiencing the same issues with the Health Connector! We need our health insurance that we paid for! Please help!"

"Tomorrow is April 1st, and I have a house full of health care issues. My wife is a cancer survivor who needs scans, my son has mental issues. I am overweight and have heart issues. We need to schedule appointments but can't since we don't have active insurance. We have prescriptions but can't fill them as we don't have insurance. This has been going on for a month."

Recovery." To ground the effort in real terms, he began his Power-Point presentation with a slide showing some examples of Connector customers' points of pain.

Louis and Vicki described their project-management approach. Over the next six weeks, through the 45-Day Plan, the team would directly attack the customer and operational problems identified in the follow-the-facts review and take actions to resolve them. Louis described the plan as ambitious but doable—and necessary. It was an urgent call for action to meet an urgent need.

Here, by staking out what would be done in forty-five days, Louis was leading with *time* to create urgency, new momentum, and energy for a team that he knew was tired and feeling a bit beaten up. The forty-five-day time clock focused everyone on the most important work to be done.

He was also demanding accountability—as a team, and for the specific deliverables. To establish a common understanding of accountability, top-level Connector staffers and key consultant contractors would be brought together as the Operations Recovery Team. To support the sense of urgency, there would be a meeting of that team and another management meeting each day, with ad hoc meetings as needed on specific topics.

The daily Operations Recovery Team meeting (aka leadership review meeting) provided an opportunity for the Connector leadership and the team to review all projects and critical performance metrics and also a time to raise new concerns. For specific projects, the leadership review allowed an objective presentation of overall project status and a discussion on progress, problems needing attention, and mitigation efforts for the hurdles ahead. Each project was presented as green (on target), yellow (issues ahead, but they appear solvable), or red (a call for leadership help). Louis told the team that he had learned long ago that an honest red status was more manageable than an optimistic (or deceptive) yellow or green.

While the accomplishments of a project with green status were noted, the leadership review prioritized time for yellow and red items. In these Operations Recovery meetings, it wasn't enough to raise issues. The team needed to determine what action was required to help move each one to green. With everyone in the room, Louis or Vicki could assign team members to next steps and set specific deadlines for completion. Those next steps might include a meeting of key principals in a few hours, an update on an IT systems enhancement, or a decision that would involve Louis and others. It was an organized way to translate urgency into progress and results.

After the leadership review of the project portfolio, Louis or Vicki would lead a round-the-table discussion in which everyone in the room would have an opportunity to speak. There was no hierarchy. Each person's perspective was considered important. Every voice was expected to be heard. It was a chance to ask a question of leadership, point out a connection, or identify new issues. Something was always learned in the round-the-table discussion that might not otherwise have been revealed. It could be the moment when it became clear that the handoff between key functions was missing, or the realization that completing one task was critical for multiple key actions to follow. But there were also moments of applause when the team reported breakthroughs—when complex tech and operational changes worked as planned and cleared thousands of customer issues in short order.

Project Management: Answer the Phones!

One of the first priorities the team was to address was the thousands of people who had called with questions about their health-care coverage. Performance metrics showed that four of every ten calls to the call center were abandoned by callers who just gave up after waiting. Unfortunately, although surviving the wait typically meant that contact had been made between the caller and the call center, it did not mean that the customer's problem was solved. Without intervention, the performance of the call center threatened to only get worse.

The call center typified the problems plaguing the Connector. It was operated by consultants who were managed by the Connector staff. Providing basic call-center services wasn't exactly breaking new ground—examples of call centers that provided outstanding service were easy to find. Getting this one to work would create some sense of stabilization for the overall operation and would demonstrate what was possible with other core functions.

Louis requested an emergency meeting with the leadership of the consultancy responsible for the call center. Within about thirty-six hours, two executives and a small team had flown in from various cities around the country and were arranged at one end of a table in one of the Connector's spartan conference rooms. A few members of the Connector staff involved in the management of the call center joined, along with Vicki and Steve. When everyone was seated, Louis walked somberly into the room and sat at the head of the table. Firmly and directly, he called on the consultants to bring their best-in-class experts from anywhere in the world to evaluate what had happened and to develop the interventions to turn this fiasco around. He invoked their contractual responsibility and reminded them of the real harm caused by poor performance—to working people who could not access health insurance any other way and paid for their coverage with their own money. After a short discussion, the consultants committed top people and resources.

Within days, their new team had arrived. Along with Vicki and the Connector staff, they reviewed everything connected with the call center, including personnel numbers, hours of service, recruitment, training, and key reference materials. In brief, the analysis showed that the staffers in place were insufficient to handle call volume and lacked suitable training, and the source materials they used to answer callers' questions were out of date and sometimes even inaccurate. Vicki identified the lack of accurate information as a major communications breakdown among all the parties involved, including the other consultants and the Connector team.

She and the consultants developed a project plan. It was rigorously monitored at the Operations Recovery Team's daily meetings. More personnel were hired for the call center. A new training curriculum was developed. New protocols for handling calls and tracking issues were implemented. IT system improvements were tested and rolled out. Regular communications among all parties involved were established, along with a clear path for escalating issues. The tough project-management approach—with its firm deadlines supported by fast problem resolution—worked. By the second week of April, the abandoned-call rate was below 3 percent, and the average speed to answer was less than sixty seconds.

Conquering IT and Collecting Data

By the time call-center performance had been stabilized, the number of people with problems related to the recent open enrollment was in the tens of thousands and growing daily. So were calls to the governor's office. Discrepancies in one issue alone—accurate date-of-birth—exceeded 10,000. The Operations Recovery Team took a follow-the-facts approach. A small group of staff and consultants analyzed each instance to determine the issue, the cause, and the impact. That intense evaluation of thousands of individual cases was completed in several days. Closer examination revealed patterns, so the team established three main categories of problems. That allowed it to prioritize the specific project work needed.

Relentless, incremental progress

Louis directed that top priority be given to cases in which an insurance-coverage issue put customers and their families at some risk: a surgery was scheduled, or a family member was ill and coverage was unclear, even though the customer believed that the premium had been paid.

Next were fixes to the IT system so that it could perform functions that were not working as intended. Literally hundreds of issues had been identified. Each one caused problems that would potentially affect customers' coverage. Those issues that had the greatest impact on the most customers and would provide critical information to the call center to proactively address problems would be prioritized.

The third category involved reconciling customers' payments and accounts. In some instances, health insurance coverage was in place, but the billing and payments were wrong. There were thousands of cases of underpayment or overpayment with customers waiting for refunds. Louis instructed the team to evaluate which of these problems needed an IT systems fix and which needed a policy change. He led the discussions to prioritize changes that affected the most people and ensure that individuals weren't penalized for an error made by the Connector.

Progress was tracked daily at both the individual-transaction and the systems-performance levels. For example, individual customer problems were monitored to see that issue was resolved and the customer was satisfied. At a systems level the team focused on the quality of the data exchange between IT platforms to rapidly identify and fix issues in order to reduce system-wide errors.

All this added up to relentless, incremental progress that would improve and eventually stabilize the entire program. *Measure. Evaluate. Adjust. Repeat!* had become core practice. We began to see real positive impact for the families served by the Connector.

Rapid-Release Approach

The first 45-Day Plan for Operations Recovery was followed by another to further steady the Connector's functions. Simultaneously, work progressed toward the complex operations and systems changes that needed to be in place for the approaching open enrollment.

Because of their shared technology platforms, the changes needed involved MassHealth, the state's Medicaid program, and the 1.7 million lives it covered as well as to the Health Connector itself. In the ramp up to the implementation of the Affordable Care Act, state health officials had decided that a single front door for eligibility for both entities was desirable. A common portal was seen as both customer-oriented and helpful to the management of both programs. However, the difficulties in implementing this design decision (and other policy choices) were widely underestimated. While strategically linking the two programs appeared to be good policy, it meant that problems with the Connector would also affect the much larger MassHealth program, potentially putting billions of dollars of federal matching funds at risk.

To coordinate the intricate systems changes needed, a senior-level committee was established, including leaders from the Connector, MassHealth, and the state's central IT agency. Staffed by Patricia Wada, this committee determined the rollout of system enhancements. Its work required a deep understanding of the various components of the IT system and their implications for real-life operations. The committee had much to do, both to rectify the situation at the Connector and to address some critical systems capabilities for MassHealth.

Louis and Patricia had proposed that a series of releases every six to eight weeks would provide actual improvements faster and more effectively than a single big-bang approach just before the next open enrollment. The coordinating committee agreed. The rapid-release approach was another example of the importance of leading with time in the project-planning triangle of *time, scope,* and *resources.* Though each release had involved significant testing, when implementing dozens of changes, from the test environment to actual production, some new issues invariably emerged. Then quick fixes were immediately developed, tested, and implemented prior to the next release. For example, Release 5.0, with more than a dozen major enhancements, went live in early May. Release 5.1 followed just a few weeks later and focused on error resolution and repairing defects from recent fixes. These short-cycle releases created a continual stream of enhanced functionality, which provided steady improvement in services. It also built confidence.

Competing interests among state agencies and consultant contractors made the plan ripe for disaster. Instead, the committee had frank discussions about priorities and resources. Each member of the coordinating committee took responsibility for understanding the perspectives of the others; each demonstrated a willingness to defer their own agency's priorities for a greater need. This wasn't easy. It was bumpy and contested. But it worked.

Test. Evaluate. Fix. Then Do It Again!

As we have noted, the success of every major technology implementation, upgrade, or enhancement has two parts: the technology itself and the operational services. Technology does not exist in isolation. Changes in IT, especially if they are significant or part of a new service, require adaptations in operational processes, clarity about new information transfers and handoffs, and enough people to handle the change. Too many fix-it efforts focus on the technology and neglect operations. Another disastrous open enrollment was simply not acceptable.

Louis's deep experience in major systems and operations rollouts provided many lessons. Success was about the details. To nail them required intense planning and hard execution. Testing couldn't be a onetime activity just before the implementation of an IT systems change. Several layers of it were needed, including both the technology and the operations changes, to prove the results or to show what problems were still outstanding—before the systems release.

For complex IT projects, all the players had to be on the same page with testing protocols, data exchanges, and other interfaces. That would require an extraordinary level of collaboration. Inherent in successful collaborations is the trust that comes from working together. The Operations Recovery Team and the objective project-management approach provided new, constructive ways of working together. They began to bring positive results. Implementation of the common testing and quality-assurance plan, with its intricate detail and precise time windows, would succeed only with the coordinated participation of all parties.

In September, although I had been receiving regular updates from Steve, I wanted to know firsthand where things stood in the final couple of months before the Connector open enrollment went live. We set up a meeting for Karyn and me in the same room where the Cabinet met. No windows. No frills. Complete attention on the subject at hand. Louis guided the presentation, and I fired away with my questions. Karyn and I could see that a team was standing with Louis. It wasn't just the well-put-together PowerPoint presentation. We expected that. It was the clarity with which each speaker described their part in the overall operation.

Many topics were discussed at that meeting, but the approach to testing stood out. The team had developed a testing and quality-assurance plan for "preliminary eligibility," a process that was required to precede the formal open-enrollment period. That dress rehearsal before the big show worked.

The lessons learned included full engagement of all parties working together, thorough quality-assurance reviews, and the power of

Tech Success Needs Operations Success

Tips Tools and Tactics

For most of us, tech is ubiquitous in our daily lives through many different channels—with access anywhere, anytime, with speedy response. But, frankly, the public sector is a few steps behind. Caution rules with good reason. The government technology project landscape is littered with missed deadlines, bumpy rollouts, and baffling processing errors, not to mention outright project failure wasting millions of taxpayer dollars. Any major change worth doing is hard. Initiatives that involve tech introduce added complexities. Further, in the delivery services provided only by the public sector, while we know that good results mean vast improvement, failure is not an option. In the spirit of lessons learned, we offer this advice:

1. **Tech might be the answer, but first define the problem.** Take the time to look at the facts and determine the problem to solve—and then explore what to do and how to do it. Tech alone is rarely the remedy. Take the time to understand how tech is part of the solution package.

2. **Be smart about procurement.** The biggest problem with most government IT procurements is they take too long. Too often, by the time the bid is drafted, finalized, advertised, responded to, and an award is made, the technology has changed and the bid is obsolete. The second biggest problem is the tendency to build something versus buying a

proven product, or when renting on someone else's platform is a better answer. Leverage the work of those who have gone through the bleeding edge of development—proving stability, security, and scalability. Optimize these products to meet your needs. And procure with urgency.

3. **Good tech needs good operations, and vice versa.** A successful tech component needs an equally successfully operations component. The opposite is also true. A "win" in one area but not the other is only a half result. How tech works and how ops works must be one. One team (and make sure that you have the people—both operations and tech—to enable success). One common goal. One implementation plan. One set of performance metrics.

4. **Get legal help.** In the public sector, laws and regulations define who to serve, eligibility requirements, and even terms (i.e., What's a household?). Especially with initiatives that involve multiple agencies, these important definitions can be complex or even potentially conflicting. Ask your legal team to provide full consideration of the legal requirements and to provide options that are breakthroughs, not barriers.

5. **Don't take short cuts.** Test and pilot. Insist on full testing protocols as appropriate to the project that includes quality assurance, production-run simulation, and volume testing. Run pilots of the developing functionality with real users and immediately incorporate the feedback to address key problems. Ensure that training materials, operations manuals, and documentation are continually updated.

(continued)

6. **Overprepare for the rollout.** Confirm complete staff training. Check equipment. Provide an internal help desk. Ready communications rollout. Set up a fast, problem-escalation response team. And if a bit more time is needed for testing or the rollout, take a breath and give the team a few days. Better to be a little later than planned than to shake public confidence with a botched rollout.

"production-like" testing to find and correct faults before full production. Louis insisted on including that kind of testing as part of the full protocol. Production-like testing is a full-scale simulation of functionality, with imperfect data like that in real life. Such a test puts a system through its paces at full volume, either showing that it functions as planned or revealing all the bugs that need to be fixed. All the parties at this meeting committed to create a joint plan for integration handoffs among their separate systems and to act and implement as a single-delivery team.

Reaching out

As spring moved into summer, the successful implementation of the forty-five-day plans and numerous IT systems upgrades provided a sense of stability in the basic operations. Customer issues had been resolved. Incoming calls and requests were readily handled. Regular systems testing demonstrated that the past issues had been addressed and that new features and capabilities were working.

The Massachusetts Health Connector was established to expand health-care coverage, especially for those who were not being served or had difficulty finding affordable health insurance. The purpose, of course, is what government services are all about. Even though Massachusetts led all the states with the highest percentage of people insured—almost 97 percent—it was estimated that several hundred thousand people had no health insurance of any kind. That's a lot of people left out of the health-care system. Thus, the open enrollment had twin goals: a functioning system and an increase in the number of residents covered. Louis, the management team, and the new board were determined that it would achieve both.

A robust outreach effort was launched to target underserved communities. The number of customer centers doubled to six locations across the state, and the team expanded the capacity of local groups to reach out to individuals. A media campaign supported those efforts. This was the first comprehensive effort by my administration to reach out to communities often left out of government services. It served as a model going forward.

"A Striking Turnaround"

As the 2015 open enrollment moved from November into December, I watched the effort of the previous eight months pay off. The new website was taking in hundreds of thousands of applications and making appropriate eligibility determinations for both the Connector and MassHealth. The call center's performance was strong, and the outreach program was attracting previously underserved customers. More than 36,000 new people were enrolled. Although glitches occurred, the overall customer experience was smooth and received high marks in surveys.

No news means good news. From a media perspective, though, it was boring. A December 23 headline from the news service MassLive captured the positive results: "Massachusetts Health Connector enrollment goes smoothly for 2016." For the Connector, after a couple of years of very tough press, a straightforward, low-key media story was in fact a tribute to the team's hard work.

In December 2015, I was happy with the calm reception in the press. But on March 12, 2019, four years after Louis's announcement of the first recovery plan, I held a press conference at the Health Connector's offices regarding the open enrollment that had just ended in late January. It was the third one for Louis, his team, and the new board. They deserved credit, and I wanted to make sure they got it. Not only had the enrollment gone smoothly, but we were able to report the largest membership in the Connector's thirteen-year history. A *Boston Globe* headline reported: "Sign-ups Surge on Mass. Health Connector." The story began, "Five years ago, the Massachusetts Health Connector was broken. People couldn't sign up for coverage online. Exhausted employees at the state-run insurance exchange used paper to enroll people, but they couldn't keep up with demand. A striking turnaround has taken place."[4]

The March 2019 total membership of 282,000 Massachusetts residents included 65,000 new members, half of them from the communities we'd targeted because of their lower rates of insurance coverage. The open-enrollment results were being heralded as the best in the nation. Step by step, the Connector had gone from "worst" to "first."

The positive news continued for the 2020 open enrollment. At a media event on February 16, 2020, Louis and Health and Human Services Secretary Marylou Sudders announced another significant increase in membership of 57,000, providing a total of 312,000 Massachusetts residents with access to affordable health care through the Connector. Louis noted that the Connector offered the lowest premiums of any exchange in the nation. That announcement was one of the last bright lights before the fury of the Covid-19 pandemic.

On April 12, 2021, the fifteenth anniversary of the Massachusetts law that created the Health Connector, Karyn and I had a chance to celebrate the Connector's accomplishments at a media event at a Worcester community health center. The main purpose of the press conference was to provide a Covid-19 update, but we also wanted to feature the Connector on this landmark day. It was a proud, positive moment.

As governor, I have come to understand that it's important for me, and for other public-sector leaders, to celebrate successes when they occur. That puts wind in the sails of the team. It creates or accentuates momentum. And it helps to restore faith in government—in the idea that it can work for the people.

. . .

We tell this story because it captures all four elements of the Results Framework—*people*, *facts*, *how*, and *results*. The Massachusetts Health Connector case highlights what can be achieved by focusing on a combination of new leadership and existing talent to create a turnaround team. The actions taken to align accountability from top to bottom, not just by bringing in a new CEO but by shaking up the board, put a much-needed spotlight on governance. Prioritizing the customer experience to drive project selection and ultimately measuring the results provided an essential foundation for determining what to do. And a key lesson for how to do it came from ensuring that technology projects did not relate to hardware and software alone but were part of the overall processes and systems. For change to be successful, all the parts and pieces of the system need attention. This story also highlights the importance and the intricacy of working with consultants. Finally, intense adherence to a project-management approach meant that significant improvements were made in timely and effective ways. And such results matter, to real people in need.

Managing a Recovery

Transportation

t was Snowmageddon—the ninety-plus inches of snow that smothered the metro Boston region in the winter of 2015 and knocked out the MBTA, the public transit system known as the T. Although it was the target of constant complaint, we all put up with the MBTA, which provided more than 1.2 million rides each day. When the agency announced a shutdown due to the snow, it delivered a gut punch to the community and the economy.

Many residents couldn't get to work, doctor's appointments, and essential services. The engines of our economy—the dozens of colleges and universities, the top-rated hospitals and research facilities, and the nationally known financial companies—closed or slow-walked their daily business, which in turn affected all the smaller shops dependent on their commerce. A news report from WBZ-TV made it personal: "We rushed to take the bus and now we have to walk the rest of the way," a woman told a CBS Boston reporter. "It's exhausting walking in the snow." She was forced to walk the two-plus miles from Kenmore Square to Mass General Hospital.

While we addressed the immediate recovery of the MBTA from the winter of 2015 (see chapter 4), the terrible snows did us a favor by clearly exposing the deep and pervasive problems at the T. The total transit failure called attention to the urgent question of what it would take to ensure a viable, reliable MBTA.

If my first major test as governor was the snow emergency itself, the next was what to do with the MBTA, the fifth-largest mass transit system in the nation. How should we react when our public transportation lifeline failed? This wasn't a single broken thing that could be fixed simply. The problems had been building for years. And now delivered a crippling blow to how we lived, worked, and got around the Boston area.

At that time, I had no authority over the MBTA. By statute, it was a stand-alone authority, responsible to the board of directors of the Massachusetts Department of Transportation. It did not report to the secretary of transportation or to me. Over the years, several reports had described long-standing problems at the MBTA, but little had changed.

Yes, the governor made appointments to its board of directors. But it would be months before my first appointment and years before my appointments to the board were the majority. Yet here was a crisis.

A few members of my staff, wearing their political hats, warned me off. So did others, including some in the legislature. They reasoned:

- It was not my problem. There was a separate board over which I had no control.

- The MBTA wasn't fixable. There was a reason that so little had changed, even after the problems had been highlighted. The status quo had successfully fended off any meaningful reform.

- Once I got involved, I would be stuck with this
  issue—*forever.*

I paused and thought about the whole situation. I disagreed on the first two points and acknowledged the third. To the first point, this was indeed my problem. Though the MBTA was technically a stand-alone entity, this had happened on my watch. No one other person could take the lead. Not to act was to duck responsibility.

To the second point, I knew both that the MBTA had significant shortcomings and that I didn't know the extent of its problems. But I believed they could be addressed. The results wouldn't come fast, but they had to come. It's said, "Never waste a crisis." Here was a crisis, and here was an opportunity.

To the third point, I agreed. The MBTA and I would be stuck with each other for as long as I was in office, and the legacy of what we did or didn't do would follow me afterward.

An immediate recovery of the public transit system from the snow emergency had to be the first order of business. Simultaneously, we needed a plan to address the long-standing problems at the MBTA.

A Hard-Nosed Evaluation

We needed a no-holds barred evaluation. The MBTA couldn't do a self-assessment with lame-duck leadership and an entrenched bureaucracy. Dumping more and more money into the system when customers riding the bus, commuting by train, or taking the subway faced increasingly frustrating experiences was a nonstarter. We needed an outside view in. The work had to be done quickly and objectively. It had to be unassailable on a factual basis, not linked to financial or other special interests.

We always start with *people*. Who were the best ones for this critical job at this critical moment? After discussions with my team, I decided to charge a distinct group with diagnosing the problems and making recommendations. The stakes were high. Previous reports took up space on shelves. Any bold recommendation, even if backed up by facts, needed to withstand tremendous public scrutiny and attack from all corners, from labor unions to transportation advocates. This group needed to provide a basis for strong action by both the administration and the legislature, because some critical changes were bound to require new laws.

On February 20, with the winter recovery efforts underway, I called for a special panel to review the MBTA. Too often in the public sector, establishing a commission is an artful deflection that results in no action beyond a report. But I was establishing this panel with the intention of acting on its advice. The people selected to review the MBTA affirmed its importance. They had been involved with administrations at the local, state, and national levels. I wanted to emphasize not only that the group I had picked had deep experience and was nonpartisan, but also that its members' experience went beyond Massachusetts. We needed to change the dynamics of the status quo. Following past procedures would only yield the same unacceptable results.

In the end, the panel consisted of three nationally recognized experts in transportation and three locally recognized experts, including a former head of the Federal Highway Administration, a former CEO of the New York Metropolitan Transportation Authority, an internationally recognized policy expert, and a local mayor. I asked our new secretary of transportation, Stephanie Pollack, to be a full participant in the panel's deliberations. I had selected Stephanie for the position because of her encyclopedic knowledge of the transportation system and her iconoclastic perspective on what needed to be done to address our most intransigent problems. A dedicated team from the governor's office and the Department of Transportation supported the group.

Typically, an effort like this would take a year or more, but as a community we couldn't wait. To emphasize the urgency, I asked for a full report by the end of March, some forty days from the panel's inception. In my formal charge to the group members, I asked them to first find and diagnose the facts and then "make recommendations to improve the MBTA's governance, structure, financials, and operations in both the short and longer terms to enable the MBTA to plan, operate, and maintain a 21st-century public transportation system." It was a call for a follow-the-facts approach to clarify the problems to be solved and develop proposals for what to do and how to do it.

The panel would meet a couple of times a week at dusk and go late into the evening. This was the administration's first full-on follow-the-facts diagnostic, including critical evidence (reports and data), firsthand points-of-pain accounts (interviews and testimony), and a get-out-of-the-tower reality (site visits and peer review). Not only did the panel members consider previous reports, but they called for presentations from an extensive list of people, including past MBTA managers and longtime transportation advocates. More than thirty major organizations provided background information and comments. The panel asked for a peer review to learn how the MBTA measured up against other transit systems, including those considered the best in the world. To gain a firsthand understanding, the group toured several MBTA maintenance and operations facilities. Its overall review included an analysis of operating costs, revenue, workforce performance, capital construction, and governance. The deep dive into the MBTA's history, present circumstances, and peer comparisons provided a strong factual basis for the panel's recommendations. The group knew it was important to learn from the past, but also to find a way forward.

The Panel's Diagnosis: Pervasive Structural Failure

We balance respect for what MBTA and Keolis (commuter rail) employees do to deliver 1.3 million daily rides, using out-of-date equipment, with a recognition that the MBTA system:

- Is in severe financial distress and would be insolvent without significant and continually increasing funding from the Commonwealth each year.

- Lacks a viable maintenance and repair plan for vehicles, facilities, signals, track and power systems, even though these are core responsibilities of the agency.

- Lacks a culture of performance management and accountability.

- Is governed ineffectively, in part because funding and financial responsibilities are too distant from decision makers and customers.

Some have called the winter of 2015 a "stress test" for the MBTA. While the MBTA "survived" the test, short-term costs were significant in disruption, economic losses, and public and private hardship. The long-term costs are even more troubling: the loss of public confidence in our regional transit system. The catastrophic winter breakdowns were symptomatic of structural problems that require fundamental change.

On April 8, 2015, the six-member special panel issued its report: "Back on Track—An Action Plan to Transform the MBTA." It was comprehensive and tough.

Rx for a Disabled System

The fact diagnostic showed troublesome performance in nearly every aspect of the organization. The special panel's report went on to detail nine critical areas of concern, including chronic capital under-investment, ineffective workplace practices, an unsustainable oper-ating budget, and a lack of customer focus. Its report stated: "The MBTA is not organized to operate as the customer-oriented busi-ness it is."

Poor financial management ran from the top all the way through the operations of the organization. Operating costs per vehicle rev-enue mile, a key performance metric, were the second highest among all peer agencies and growing at twice the rate of inflation. At the same time, the panel recognized that we were missing new revenue that could be generated from advertising, parking, real estate, and other non-passenger activity, leaving tens of millions of dollars unre-covered annually.

An important measure of any transportation system is the con-dition of its physical infrastructure and what it costs to have that equipment and those facilities in a state of good repair. We knew that the MBTA was old and needed help. The special panel's report was not the first to point out significant deficiencies in its capital infra-structure. However, with this report, we as a community realized that what we understood as a problem was just the tip of the iceberg. The report estimated that an eye-popping $7 billion would be required just to maintain existing capital infrastructure and equipment.

Not to modernize. Not to be more climate-resilient or reduce carbon emissions. Not to expand services. Just to maintain.

To add insult to injury, the MBTA was not spending the capital funds the Legislature had already authorized. In the previous five years—despite a massive underinvestment in its vehicles, facilities, safety systems, and railways—it had spent only $2.3 billion of the $4.5 billion planned for capital construction and maintenance.

It wasn't just poor financial and capital investment performance that was so pervasive. The lack of overall management was evident throughout. For example, the panel's report noted, the MBTA's absenteeism rate was a stark outlier. Whereas the Bureau of Labor Statistics reported a 3 percent absentee rate for the transportation industry as a whole, and other transit agencies reported rates of 5 to 6 percent, the MBTA's rate was 11 to 12 percent. The impact on customers was significant. Tens of thousands of bus trips were canceled each year owing to unplanned absences.

The report also underscored a pernicious lack of accountability. Although the board had presumably been set up to be insulated against short-term politics by stretching appointments across multiple years and gubernatorial terms, it was accountable to no one. Furthermore, it had wide responsibility beyond the MBTA, including Massachusetts highways and the Registry of Motor Vehicles. A big job for a vital set of services. However, the board met only monthly, and less often during the summer. In the best of circumstances, that was not often enough to oversee three large agencies.

What to do?

In the end, the special panel delivered nineteen recommendations for the administration and ten for the legislature. A number of them were controversial, including one to allow private-sector vendors to provide some services.

However, the most significant proposal focused on changing the MBTA's oversight structure. The panel asserted that while its more-specific recommendations could result in some improvement, they would not be enough without a significant change in the governance structure. It reasoned that the current board of directors could not be relied upon to carry out the actions necessary to move ahead. The panel advocated for the creation of a new entity dedicated exclusively to the MBTA. It proposed the Fiscal and Management Control Board (FMCB), with oversight responsibility for all aspects of the MBTA. Acknowledging that monthly meetings were inadequate, the panel suggested weekly meetings. In a call to align responsibility and accountability, it recommended that board members be appointed by and serve coterminously with the governor. And to stress that urgent matters required urgent actions, the panel specifically recommended that the current board of directors resign. I endorsed the proposal.

With the release of the special panel's report, I requested that Secretary Stephanie Pollack draft legislation to establish the MBTA's FMCB and carry out the panel's other recommendations. I also directed Steve to request the resignation of the current board members. I could not command them to step down. We knew that this was a highly unusual move, yet absolutely necessary. A couple of months earlier, we had taken a similar course of action to address a comparable crisis at the Massachusetts Health Connector.

This time, there was no surprise when the call came, because the media had picked up on the special panel's recommendation. Nevertheless, I was grateful for each member's professionalism in respecting our request.

The day after the board agreed to step down, I submitted a proposal for MBTA reform legislation based on the special panel's report. By the end of June, the legislature had enacted a bill that closely followed the proposal. The law provided for the establishment of a newly configured Department of Transportation board and a newly created MBTA Fiscal and Management Control Board, both appointed by and coterminous with the governor; a three-year waiver of current procurement restrictions; and an imperative to address other special-panel recommendations. The legislature had acted quickly and done its part. Now it was the administration's turn.

Some joked, after barking and chasing car, dog catches car. Now what?! Others more somberly warned, be careful what you ask for. The MBTA would now be my administration's responsibility.

How to do it?

We approached filling board appointments and naming the MBTA leadership team much as we had done for cabinet and key agency lead roles. This was about knowledge and know-how, not party affiliation. I was looking for tough-minded, fact-oriented, fair, objective problem-solvers. We wanted a mix of people with public-sector and private-sector experience who would both respect and challenge the orthodoxy of how things were done. We searched for people who would respect one another and the customers and cities and towns they served. And we kept our eye on the need to reflect the stakeholders through a diverse team.

For the FMCB, we vetted several dozen candidates. As the list narrowed, I met with each of the final contenders. I needed to know that they understood the depth of the challenge and the opportunity before them. I wanted to learn more about their specific experience and thoughts about the role of transportation in our community. And I wanted to ensure that their commitment to public service was greater than any personal or political agenda.

On July 17, I announced the makeup of the five-member board with Joseph Aiello as its chair. Calm, with deep experience in finance and capital projects in the private and public sectors (including the MBTA early in his career), Aiello emphasized a fact- and results-based approach. The other members were a union labor leader, a director of a local business council, and two people with local and state financial expertise. Four days later, Chair Aiello gaveled in the first of the board's weekly meetings.

At the same time that the FMCB members were being selected, we were focused on naming the MBTA's management team. The MBTA had functioned as a relatively flat organization with thin top management. The special panel determined that a key organizational weakness was not having enough senior managers with distinct responsibilities and experience. A crucial panel recommendation called for the creation of a new position, chief administrative officer, which would focus on all things fiscal and administrative. The panel reasoned that with this executive addressing budget and administrative functions, the general manager would be free to fully focus on the capital program, customer services, and other key priorities. The third member of this senior team, the COO, would prioritize the day-to-day service operations of the trains and buses.

Note that the leadership roles for the MBTA differ from those of the Health Connector. That's as it should be. In the late nineteenth century, the architect Louis Sullivan coined the phrase "form follows function" regarding building design. The concept is just as apt for organizations and the work they need to do. In other words, the team and the effort should be designed for the particular need. Their skills and experience should match the problem to be solved. And governance, decision-making, and meetings—the core functional infrastructure—should be designed (and periodically reviewed and adjusted) to meet the demands and purpose of the organization and key initiatives.

On July 30, with support from the lieutenant governor and me, Secretary Stephanie Pollack announced the MBTA's new leadership team: Frank DePaola, general manager (sadly, since deceased after battling cancer); Brian Shortsleeve, chief administrative officer, and Jeff Gonneville, chief operating officer. Frank was an experienced transportation engineer and manager who had previously held leadership roles as the state highways administrator and at the MBTA. Brian was a businessperson I'd previously worked with. Though he did not have transportation experience, he brought a deep understanding of financial and operating issues. We had come to know Jeff during the winter emergency, when he played a pivotal role in the successful recovery effort. As the former MBTA chief mechanical officer, he understood the details of the transit operation. While the general manager remained the MBTA's overall leader, these three positions composed its senior team, combining vital knowledge of the organization with fresh, critically needed outside management experience.

After the new leader, new hires

You simply cannot fix what's broken without talent and experience. Although the organization had some truly terrific managers and staffers, it simply didn't have enough talent to meet the volume and the urgency of the work. We also believed that the MBTA needed an infusion of new people. Because they aren't part of the status quo, new hires provide a perspective that allows for fresh ways of performing the work. Our experience showed that the bigger the problem, the bigger the change in personnel needed—not just in the C-suite but at every level of the organization.

At the MBTA, although the need for additional people was apparent, it would take determination to bring them on. In insular organizations, especially older ones, laborious procedures plus internal management resistance can make for a slow, reluctant operating atmosphere. The MBTA's attitude toward change had been "No. Not now." We needed the people who would move to "Let's go. Here's how."

With the senior leadership team, Steve pushed for the development of a critical-hires list along with greater speed in hiring. Identifying the critical hires was an essential start, but it needed to be coupled with actually putting people in the jobs. At the MBTA, it typically took several weeks to write a job description, several weeks more to get it approved, and a few months to post and interview before the new hire started. The process averaged four and a half months, sometimes much longer. That had to change, and quickly.

We lent our best HR resources from the governor's office to partner with the HR teams at the Department of Transportation and the MBTA in quickly drafting job descriptions, creating a key position-tracking process, and launching a robust recruitment effort. Although it was clear that the pool for positions that required specific rail and mechanical experience was limited (search firms were engaged here), many of the roles were not unique to transportation, including procurement, finance, human resources, information technology, project management, and especially capital construction. For those, a wide net could be cast. An irony of the MBTA's well-known problems is that they helped with recruitment. Talented folks who had never considered working for the MBTA wanted to help address one of the most important issues of the day.

While a push from the outside, especially from the executive office, might be helpful, making a sustained change like this within an organization takes committed and aligned leaders. Not just the HR team, and not just one person on the leadership team, but all of top management embraced the urgency. Where time is spent reflects priorities, and senior leaders and HR folks were huddling twice weekly to secure immediate approvals, clear any obstacles, and ensure that leading prospects were interviewed quickly.

In addition, it would take a change in pay scale to keep and attract talent. Studies showed that the MBTA's management compensation was consistently below market, sometimes quite significantly. Those lower salaries made it hard to attract and retain good people. The new board prioritized the changes needed.

All in all, these HR activities were not exactly trailblazing stuff, especially for private-sector entities with thousands of employees. But this was new territory for the MBTA—and for many public-sector agencies. Within a year, the board reported, "The time to hire fell by more than 50 percent . . . with 142 designated as priority hires." Within two years, new people occupied 70 percent of the senior management positions. Every new hire and key promotion filled a known gap and helped provide the additional hands and minds needed.

Prioritizing Customers and Financial Performance

With the essential elements of people are policy in place—new leadership to help reset the effort and added team members to build upon existing staff talent—attention moved to the next part of the Results Framework: what to do and how to do it. The senior leadership team dove into selecting the issues to address and moving from concepts to results.

A former colleague and mentor used to tell me, when we were in the middle of trying to tackle our myriad problems, all of which seemed important: "You *can* do everything. Just not all at once." In a word: prioritize. For the MBTA, this meant explicitly ranking goals and setting target deadlines. Two goals topped the list: improving customer service and stabilizing financial performance.

Our focus on customers prioritized how riders were affected. The panel report noted: "The focus of the agency appears too often to be internal and not on the needs of its customers. . . . Years of unreliable service, inadequate facilities, poor communication, and lack of written customer oriented protocols have broken the bond of trust between the MBTA and its riders." But now the focus had changed from simply running buses, trains, and subway cars to serving customers by improving on-time performance, minimizing the negative impact of construction, and providing timely and accurate communications.

After some discussion of a project or other specific action, Secretary Pollack would often highlight the purpose of this work: "How does this help the customer, and how do we quantify the result?" A spotlight on customer impact drove both targets and, eventually, the review of daily performance metrics for each train, subway, bus, and ferry route. It was a results-driven approach of continual measurements and adjustments.

Financial performance, too, was a clear driver of project selection. The special panel report put a spotlight on how the lack of financial management had affected operational performance. Peer transit agencies in other cities demonstrated a more effective use of public funds. Other major public entities in Massachusetts had more-robust capital programs. While both public and private sectors in the rest of the world had for years sought cost savings and service improvements, the MBTA had not engaged.

The weak state of its financials and operations was summed up by a 50 percent increase in operating expenses over the previous eight years—with no increase in passengers—combined with hundreds of millions of dollars in unspent capital funds. We had reason to make "fiscal" the first word in the new board's name.

Facing Financial Troubles

Tips Tools and Tactics

Budget problems hurt the entire organization. The greater the problem, the greater the changes needed—and the greater the pushback from defenders of the status quo. As always, though, in crisis, there is also opportunity. Here are some of the realities we think about when addressing financial troubles:

1. **More than dollars and cents.** In any organization, but especially in the public sector, budget changes can have enormous impact on the livelihood of individuals, families, and their community. A budget exercise is not just bean counting. Refrain from one-size-fits-all thinking across the board cuts. Budget cuts or revenue opportunities are not equal. Assess the service and operational impact of possible cuts—and increases. Acknowledge not just the financial, but also the human impact of any change.

2. **One spreadsheet to rule them all.** Too often, competing budgets sprout up—a product of some combination of disputed financial responsibilities, shadow spreadsheets, and organizational turf. Get to one record of budget truth.

3. **Numbers and narrative.** Essential financial information should include a full presentation of the numbers, including appropriate units of measure (i.e., individual transaction, office, program) and trends (i.e., year-over-year, seasonal, monthly, weekly, daily). And it should also include a narrative that discusses the "so what." In other words, so what are the numbers indicating about performance, changes in circum-

stance, and trends? Knowing the numbers alone is not enough. The narrative fills out the picture.

4. **Overlooked opportunities.** Even the best managers may need some help. Here are some often overlooked areas:

   - **Purchasing and contracts.** Be sure that you are getting the best price and value on goods and services. Don't be afraid to change vendors, to ask the existing vendor for budget help, or to rebid.

   - **Revenue opportunities.** In the public sector, we typically spend a lot of time on evaluating expenditures and give scant attention to revenues (with the exception of taxes). Evaluate non-tax-revenue opportunities including advertising revenue, property leases, appropriate fees for services, and matching grants.

   - **Duplicate functions.** Do a business process analysis of internal procedures and drop duplicate and non-value-added steps—saving time and money.

5. **Peer review.** Talk to and learn how others—in your agency, other jurisdictions, and comparable-sized organizations (large nonprofits, businesses)—are achieving savings or revenues and improving performance. Copy what works. In this case, the sincerest form of flattery is also good for the pocketbook.

6. **Respect for the change process.** Engage with all those impacted, including staff, managers, and customers. Explain why the change is needed, what is involved, and its timing. Give folks the training needed to accommodate changes in operations procedures, IT applications, and customer service. Be prepared to listen—and make adjustments.

A Reset of the Operating Paradigm

With key people in place, detailed facts defining the problems, and significant initiatives underway, a project-management approach would define *how to do it*. Key projects would be evaluated as being (a) on time and on track; (b) exhibiting problems of scope or time frame that the project team would be able to handle; or (c) requiring a call for help from the senior leadership team. The agenda for leadership meetings centered on this progress review, especially to identify impediments and resolve them as quickly as possible.

Early lessons emerged from projects that had started slowly and showed little progress. An informal, modified Checklist to Green (see chapter 3) became part of the leadership team's review. Early on, the senior team identified some common stumbling blocks. *People*: Is there a dedicated lead? A dedicated core team? Have the critical hires been made? What additional resources are necessary, and what's the plan for securing them? *Governance*: Is accountability across units defined? Is it clear who is making the decision and whose input is crucial? *Legal*: Have we thoroughly reviewed all the state, federal, and contractual obligations to identify potential legal problems, and what are the options for addressing them? *Metrics*: What are the performance metrics for success? Do they measure what's important to the customer? This attention to the checklist questions meant that projects were launched with a greater likelihood of success. For projects underway that were struggling, the checklist review provided a practical analytic for getting them back on track.

As well as bringing a strong project-management approach, *how to do it* provided an opportunity to invoke best practices for how the MBTA worked. In fact, simply adopting good practices would be a huge step for an agency that was mired in habits from the 1980s.

The technology revolution had bypassed the MBTA, which had fallen prey to the status quo. For example, procurement for many items often involved multiple steps and approvals—including manually carrying hard-copy purchase orders from one location to another for signatures. Getting out of the tower would be fundamental to finding a new way forward.

Every Monday afternoon, for four hours or longer, the MBTA leadership would be front and center at the FMCB meeting. Aiello chaired those meetings, which were open to the media, typically by starting with public comment, heralding a new era of transparency and accountability. All major projects and changes in service and operations would need the new board's approval.

Overall, this focus on how drove a reset of the MBTA's operating paradigm that was supported by a strong, dedicated board aligned with the secretary and the governor. The call was to evaluate every part of the business through the lenses of fiscal responsibility, customer service, and best practice—and to do so with urgency.

Ongoing Problems, a Fresh Approach

The previous couple of decades had seen many efforts to reform the MBTA. Every few years, some combination of a blistering report and new legislation attempted to address the ongoing problems. Now we had another report and a law. We believe that what was different this time was the approach—the principles of the Results Framework. We just described the approach to people, choosing the work on the basis of facts, and an emphasis on how, with the foundation of strong governance and project management. Now let's look at two examples in practice: fiscal management and capital construction.

The power of *and*

Named the agency's first-ever chief administrative officer, Brian Shortsleeve had a job that included all things financial and administrative. He went right to work hiring a new CFO and new leaders for much of the financial team. Same with HR. The experience of the new managers brought new energy to those critical functions.

Immediately, the new finance team conducted the first comprehensive review in decades of the MBTA's budget and operations. The review confirmed the depth and scope of the problem: in 2015, operating expenses were climbing annually at a rate three times as fast as dedicated annual revenues. Projections were that $242 million more would be needed in two years to fill the budget gap, and that the deficit would climb to $427 million annually in five years.

The goal was to bend the operating-expense curve to be no greater than the revenue curve—without affecting core services. Peer comparisons showed the potential. In fact, during this period, the MBTA expanded its daily operations by adding new early-morning bus service on key routes, implementing a new Silver Line bus service to underserved areas, and increasing the number of commuter-rail passenger cars and trips. We referred to this as the power of *and*. Rather than choosing between two goals, the power of *and* incorporated both.

Many things worked. Some things didn't, such as the automated fare collection initiative. Launched in 2017 with new people, a dedicated team, and adequate funding, this hoped-for transformation for tracking both fares and passengers' travel information was a bust on its first release. It suffered from technological overreach and had problems regarding how it would be operationalized. By the end of 2020, it was clear that the project required a major reset, involving a project leadership change, rescoping, more time, and more money.

Resist Binary Choices

As you begin to focus on the goals of an initiative, what and how to tackle the problem to solve, don't settle for the false choice of "or," which pits important objectives in opposition to each other. Yes, it's easier to focus on a single result, but it too often doesn't satisfactorily address the need. Reach for "and." This can create transformative dynamics.

- **Boycott the use of "or."** Frame things with twin goals: making things better *and* saving costs. Quality *and* speed. Simplified internal processes *and* improved customer service.

- **Challenge the team to embrace *and*.** Ask the team to step beyond traditional thinking and meet the challenge to succeed at two goals. Allow that there will be some skepticism but push creativity. Ask the team what it would take to get this done and how to overcome the impediments.

- **Flip the paradigm of "why not" into "this is how."** Take discussions that previously had only one goal and unleash a different set of approaches. For example, IT with improved security *and* improved access. HR with faster hiring time cycles *and* more diverse candidates. Expanding programs to serve more people in half the time *and* no misuse of funds.

- **Acknowledge the challenge to the status quo.** Undoubtedly the challenge of "and" will mean changes to how things are currently done. A change may be as relatively simple as adding or dropping some steps in an existing process, or as profound as moving from paper to the web. Provide the resources and support for the transition.

In two years, the overall results were promising. MBTA revenues exceeded annual operating expenses for the first time in decades. Tens of millions of dollars previously designated for operating expenses could go to critical capital investments. In short, the new approach helped implement good business practices that resulted in significant financial efficiencies and improved ways of doing the work.

The capital program

In 2015, available funds could not be spent, project delivery was bottlenecked, and little existed in the planning pipeline. The MBTA capital program languished and needed an overhaul.

When the longtime lead for capital projects retired, a new team was assembled to reenergize the capital program. It quickly put together a comprehensive list of projects, both underway and in the planning stages. The initial review showed that unless action was taken to speed up ongoing projects and increase the project pipeline, the dismal results in the capital program would continue. It was a classic example of not managing what hadn't been measured.

The existing process showed little coordination among the numerous players needed to get the work done. As a result, it was at best painfully slow and, at worst, simply unproductive. Taking a strong project-management approach, the team, which included people from across the agency, met to look at each project, rapidly identify problems, and take action to resolve them. In the past, these decisions would have taken weeks or months of meetings, and further delays would be inevitable when one of them was canceled or postponed. Now all the key players were at the meeting. Follow-up was immediate. Engineering provided a date for signoff on a design. Legal prioritized a contract review. Operations assigned staff members to confirm and coordinate the service impacts. Finance noted the funding source. The governor's office followed up on permits requiring approval by an outside agency. What the capital projects team couldn't address was immediately raised to the senior leadership team.

The coordinated approach made great strides. The special-panel report had indicated that the annual "state of good repair" spending for the prior seven years averaged $389 million. In its first two years, the new team nearly doubled that figure to just over $700 million.

Progress was certainly made, but more needed to be done. The goal was to achieve a $2 billion annual capital program to meet crucial infrastructure repairs and upgrades after years of underinvestment. We wanted to deliver a generation's worth of capital improvements in a handful of years.

We had made changes in the capital construction team's leadership, supported the effort with new people resources, developed a detailed fact list of where the problems were, and instituted comprehensive leadership reviews with progress status tracking (green, yellow, red) of dozens of specific projects. Yet, this wasn't enough. This critical initiative for the success of the MBTA needed a project reset.

In 2019, realizing what $2 billion annual capital spending would mean for the MBTA's customers provided a unifying focus for its leadership team. Steve Poftak had just been named the new general manager in January. By May, he had assembled a new team, including a new chief administrative officer, and elevated a new chief of capital projects to the senior leadership group. Over the previous few years, the MBTA had made significant progress in meeting many of its fiscal targets. However, the capital program, while growing, had still not achieved its spending goals.

Throughout early 2019, in meetings with Steve Poftak and Stephanie Pollack, I reinforced the importance of the capital program to the MBTA's ultimate success. In May 2019, after the MBTA reported that it was not going to meet capital spending goals, I addressed the media to point out that unlike many other public-sector problems, this was not about a lack of funding. An $8 billion capital plan had identified funds for the next five years. The MBTA's current problem, I noted, was an inability to actually organize and spend the money. Real progress had been made. Now the capital program would need to be brought to the next level.

Poftak identified the two key problems that needed addressing: (1) hiring the staff necessary to do the work, and (2) confronting the status quo bureaucratic ways of doing business. The senior team quickly engaged.

To meet both immediate and longer-term staffing needs, a workforce planning effort completed a cross-organization review of the positions required to implement the capital program, from project managers to additional legal staffers, and then worked with the Office of Diversity to ramp up recruitment and hiring.

To tackle the internal bureaucracy, a team that was focused on process streamlining halved the number of signature approvals (conservatively estimated to save at least two weeks *per document*) and developed new standardized construction-contract templates, significantly reducing the time spent for all involved.

These improvements helped accelerate the capital program. But the tremendous growth needed would not be possible without a major change in how construction was performed.

Up to this point, most construction occurred during the hours when the MBTA was not providing service—typically late at night or just before dawn—with significant parts of that window allocated to construction setup and takedown. If crews had more uninterrupted time in which to do the work, the entire project would be accomplished much faster. To enable that, the MBTA's management proposed longer times for station and track closures and substituting buses for trains during those construction periods. In addition, and unexpectedly, Covid-19 brought a rare lemonade-out-of-lemons moment. With ridership severely down, expanding the bus-for-subway service became even more feasible, allowing for longer periods of construction. Ultimately, FY2020 capital expenditures closed out at a record $1.7 billion, with the $2 billion goal now in sight.

Saving a Project That Had Gone off the Tracks

Perhaps the mismanagement of the MBTA's premier capital project, the Green Line Extension, should have come as no surprise, given the problems running throughout the MBTA. But it was a surprise, nevertheless. The Green Line Extension was a decades-long-awaited, seven-station, 4.7-mile extension of this subway line from Cambridge into the communities of Somerville and Medford.

In January 2015, just at the end of Governor Patrick's administration, the Federal Transit Administration announced a $1 billion grant to cover half the Green Line Extension's anticipated $2 billion total cost. Hundreds of millions of dollars had already been spent or committed for the project. The federal funds were expected to pay for a significant portion of outstanding expenses. But just a few months in advance of the actual award, the budget blew up. About the same time that the special panel issued its report, we learned from Secretary Pollack that the MBTA's new estimates had leaped above $3 billion—a $1 billion increase that came with little confidence that it wouldn't go higher. The feds put the release of their funds on hold.

General Manager DePaola conducted an evaluation of what could be trimmed to lower costs. The rough estimates of $200 million to $400 million in savings would not be enough. We sought a top-to-bottom review to determine all options. The team had measured the results; now it needed to evaluate the situation and make the necessary adjustments, which would loop all the way back through the Results Framework.

We knew that this effort would require a major change in the project's leadership and the team. Pollack recruited an experienced big-projects leader and established a planning team. Additional expert resources were brought in to evaluate everything from design to construction methods. Then the focus was on delivery.

By May 2016, a total project budget of $2.3 billion was presented to the MBTA's board, including both cost savings and new funding sources. The savings would come from a simpler redesign of stations, the maintenance facility, and pedestrian and bike amenities. A design-build construction method was expected to lower costs and protect quality.

An estimated minimum of $225 million in new funds would be needed, to come from two sources. The proposal called for $150 million in federal dollars that were reserved for other projects to be reallocated to the Green Line Extension. In addition, the cities of Cambridge and Somerville would be asked to provide a total of $75 million, since both communities were expected to benefit greatly from the increased property-tax base generated by the project.

One important aspect of *how* would be the management of the project. Along with a review of the project revisions and budget estimates, the quality of the implementation team was a critical factor in the federal government's evaluation to approve its $1 billion. We had to demonstrate that we had a capable leader and a dedicated team in place. A national search found someone with proven experience on complex transportation projects, and hiring began to fill out the project-dedicated team.

Two years after the initial budget-busting news, on April 4, 2017, the federal government approved a new cost estimate of $2.3 billion and released funding. The construction market responded enthusiastically with several strong proposals. Not only was the winning bid below projected budget, but it included all six optional elements that had been eliminated to save costs. Final federal approval came on December 21, 2017, with completion of the project anticipated four years later. As of fall 2021, not only were the new stations expected to open in the coming year, but the project was running a budget surplus allowing for the repayment of funds to Cambridge and Somerville and then some.

. . .

In the summer of 2021, six years after the Fiscal and Management Control Board's first meeting, major advances had been made in capital projects, from significant funds to prepare for winter conditions, to major investments in new buses, subway cars, and safety improvements, to expansion projects such as the Green Line Extension. Throughout the system, more-accurate arrival information and new apps had improved passengers' ability to know where buses and trains were and when they would arrive. And the capital construction program had grown from $631 million in FY2014 to planned spending of $2 billion in FY2022.

In addition, over a five-year period, the MBTA had saved about $800 million in operating costs. In fact, the board reported that core operating expenses had grown at a rate of 1.6 percent in that time—a fraction of the inflation rate over that same time period. In the past, those costs would typically have been offset by state subsidies, at the expense of non-transportation budget needs such as health care and education.

The team at the MBTA had come a tremendous distance. But even so, a late bus, a canceled train, or a confusing communication meant frustration. While the needed investments in capital infrastructure and operations were leading to improved performance overall, some days it seemed like two steps forward and one step back. Better was not the end goal, and it would take years more of intensive investment to achieve the world-class transit system we envisioned. However, the actions of those six years allowed the MBTA to move forward better staffed, better prepared, and better able to perform. These actions positioned the MBTA to withstand the operating challenges and the tremendous loss of ridership revenue brought on by Covid-19.

We tell this story because it demonstrates the strengths of the Results Framework in both the short and the long terms. It shows that while some things can be readily improved—such as financial management—problems that have persisted for a long time, like a lack of attention to capital maintenance and infrastructure, permit no shortcuts. They can, however, be addressed faster, better, and more effectively with this approach. We are in the middle innings of a long game, with progress made and much more work ahead. This story shows that it takes clear accountability, strong project management, dedicated top-level people and resources for each key initiative, and a continuous attention to performance to achieve success.

An Agency Turnaround

Child Welfare

I n December 2013, the seven-year-old sister of Jeremiah Oliver mentioned to school counselors that she hadn't seen her brother for some time. The following April, Jeremiah's body was found in what appeared to be a suitcase along the highway, the victim of a brutal homicide.

Jeremiah, five years old, was one of the more than 45,000 children with open cases at the Massachusetts Department of Children and Families (DCF) that year. His family had been involved with the department since 2011. Following the report of the missing child, an investigation showed that the department's social worker had not visited the child's home since May, yet monthly in-person visits were required. The three agency staff members most directly involved with this case were fired, and one other was disciplined for not following protocols.

Days after the discovery of Jeremiah's body, the commissioner of the DCF resigned, and an interim was named. In the previous month, two other children under the department's care had died.

The Jeremiah Oliver case exposed severe weaknesses at the department. Every state has an analogous agency. Similar incidents of child abuse and neglect occur throughout this nation and cross all boundaries. If Massachusetts could be proud of its leadership on many topics, child welfare was not one of them. The DCF was an agency in crisis.

Soon after Jeremiah was reported missing, the Deval Patrick administration engaged the Child Welfare League of America, a national organization based in Washington, DC, to do a comprehensive review of agency operations. At the end of May 2014, the league released its report, which found an agency rife with issues. The report did not blame the agency for Jeremiah's tragic death but did not exonerate it either. It noted that the department was serving more children than at any time in the previous two decades, and that the staffing levels and other resources had not kept up. More than sixty specific corrective actions were outlined, covering deficiencies in policies, practices, staffing, training, management, resources, and working with partners. An Associated Press headline summed up the findings: "Report on Jeremiah Oliver case: DCF needs overhaul, more resources." The article continued, "In its report, the league said DCF is understaffed and its policies and protocols largely out of date, resulting in inconsistent handling of cases across regional offices."[1] Linda Spears, the report's main author, indicated that the challenges facing the agency were endemic.

I read the Child Welfare League of America document as a gubernatorial candidate, but more important, as a citizen and as a father. The report was a clarion call to protect the Commonwealth's most vulnerable: its children. The first recommendation especially resonated with me, for I believe in a synthesis of policy and practice.[2] I believe both must come together in clearly documented training and support materials. I believe all these must work on behalf of the children. I could see that additional staffers were needed, but they alone would not be effective without changes to how the agency operated. The recommendation put the children first—and that meant the Commonwealth needed a comprehensive approach and a revision of all the supporting policy and protocols.

Throughout 2014, the department began to implement some of the league's recommendations. Modest additional funds were added to the department's budget for more social workers and technology improvements. However, other recommendations, which addressed more deeply rooted issues, languished without dramatic progress.

A Most Difficult Mission

In late 2014, during my transition from governor-elect to governor, I started laying out a new approach for DCF. I knew from my time as undersecretary, and then secretary of health and human services, when the department reported directly to me, what a difficult mission this agency had before it. Finding the right leader would be critical. The department was continuing to operate with increasing cases and too few staffers to keep up. It had suffered a heavy blow from budget cuts and staff reductions after the 2008 Great Recession and had experienced little relief since. Further, the opioid epidemic had added more cases that were increasingly complex.

The incoming health and human services secretary, Marylou Sudders, agreed that this had to be one of her top people priorities. A member of the faculty in Boston College's social work department who had had a long career in both public and private sectors leading mental health and child welfare organizations, Marylou understood both what it meant to be a social worker in the field and what it took to support good work. It wasn't long before we agreed on the best person for the job, if we could get her: Linda Spears, the author of the Child Welfare League of America report. In so many ways, Linda's work at the league over the previous year had prepared her to lead the department's turnaround. Not only did she know in detail what areas needed improvement, but she had studied the best practices of states and major cities across the country. And early in her career, she had been a social worker at the Massachusetts DCF.

After Marylou reached out to gauge her interest, I asked Linda to come to my home in Swampscott, where I was meeting potential candidates for various important posts. In our conversation, I quickly saw how clearly she understood what we faced at the department, as well as the warmth and depth of her caring. She was incredibly well versed on this topic from her experience with other states. Linda realized how hard this work would be. She had seen successes and failures around the country. I knew that she was ready to take a leadership role. I shifted from learning about Linda to selling her on the job.

On January 5, 2015, three days before my inaugural, I announced that Linda Spears would be the next commissioner of the DCF. With Sudders and Spears on board, experienced leaders would be driving changes at the department.

Commissioner Spears translated the Child Welfare League of America report into a task list that would track the department's progress on the recommendations. A push was made to equip the DCF's social workers with laptops so that they could access critical information in the field and not have to come into the office. More funds were necessary for these and other changes. Despite facing a $1 billion deficit when I took office in January, I prioritized a $73 million increase for the department that would become effective if the legislature acted on it in July. DCF made modest headway on Linda's task list through the winter and spring. Then came summer.

Three Heart-Wrenching Stories

The league's report had revealed critical baseline observations (an initial set of facts) and produced important recommendations (an outline of what to do). But we would all come to understand that the diagnostic was incomplete. In the summer of 2015, our community relived the tragedy of Jeremiah Oliver. Three heart-wrenching incidents of children involved with the department rocked the Commonwealth.

Baby Doe

On Thursday, June 25, 2015, a woman in Winthrop, a coastal town just north of Boston, made a horrid discovery. She was walking her dog along the shoreline of Deer Island when she found an object that concerned her and called 911. The Massachusetts State Police uncovered the remains of a girl of toddler age.

The news was stunning. As a community, we had not yet recovered from the loss of Jeremiah Oliver one year earlier. Now this. The hunt for more information about Baby Doe drove national news stories throughout the summer. What had happened to this innocent child would hang like a dark cloud over us all.

Jack Loiselle

Just nineteen days after the startling discovery of Baby Doe, on July 14, Jack Loiselle was taken into emergency custody at the DCF after his father called to say that the seven-year-old was unconscious. The next day, little Jack, weighing only thirty-eight pounds, was in a coma in an intensive care unit.

This was not a case of a lost child. Jack had recently attended school and had been regularly visited by DCF social workers and others. There were "eyes" on him, but he was not protected. The department's Special Investigations Unit would conduct a detailed probe to determine what happened. However, it was clear that existing protocols were not enough.

Avalena Conway-Coxon

One month later, on Saturday, August 15, Avalena Conway-Coxon was found dead in her foster home. The two-year-old, along with another child then in department custody, had suffered from heat stroke and long exposure to high temperatures. Another unspeakable tragedy, but this time in foster care. The department launched another investigation.

This was the third major incident in less than two months—*and it was on our watch.*

My one-to-one early-morning calls with Steve shifted to focus entirely on the DCF. The Child Welfare League of America report was helpful input, but it wasn't sufficient to identify all the problems that needed addressing. We saw that new leadership alone would not be adequate for the thorough turnaround required. We needed a comprehensive approach to address the changes needed at the DCF immediately.

When do you make the call to intervene in an agency's work? How can you best provide support? These are critical questions for any leader. The intensity of these child welfare tragedies only made the situation more profound

Marylou Sudders was among the most experienced members of the cabinet. She had held a number of important positions in state government, including commissioner of mental health. She was strong, smart, and someone you would want to lead in a crisis. Linda Spears was a preeminent leader in the nation regarding child welfare and protection. She was now bringing her wisdom to Massachusetts. Together, they had jumped right in, and the department was making progress on the league's recommendations. But these three tragedies signaled a deep crisis. They called for something more.

When an agency is in crisis, it needs a different kind of help. A crisis demands support beyond the capacity of the agency itself. The status quo got things to where they are, and the situation will continue unless significant changes are made. We had to turn things around.

Deep Crises Require Disruption

Linda Spears was the strong leader we needed. She was building a solid team around her. But good people with good intent need an effective approach. Now we wanted to fully invest in the Results Framework—adding dedicated resources, fact-based solutions, rigorous project management, measurement of results, and needed adjustments.

While I knew that an intervention was necessary, I also knew that it would work best if it was a point of mutual agreement. I suggested to Marylou that Steve and the Strategic Operations staff work directly with Linda Spears and her team. With her plate already overflowing with the opioid epidemic, an overhaul of the state's Medicaid program, and other issues, Marylou welcomed the help.

So did Commissioner Spears. She recognized that day-to-day operations were already fully engaging a beleaguered department. Significant change could not be achieved by simply piling more work onto already burdened managers and staffers, though many of them would be involved in the transformation effort. New and greater resources would be needed to drive change. And to be effective, the change would require altering the approach to the work.

In discussions with Steve, Linda quickly endorsed disciplined project management supported by a dedicated team. She recognized that the overall approach would show us what was working and what needed adjustment and would provide quick identification of impediments and their solutions.

The project management team would be led by the DCF's current chief of staff, who moved full-time into that role. In the governor's office, we engaged staffers from the Strategic Operations Team and the legal office. A consultant team provided key additional support.

Led by the commissioner, a small steering committee would guide the overall effort. That group included Lian Hogan, the deputy director for operations, and key department leaders, along with the undersecretary of health and human services. Spears had just named Lian as her number two because of her deep experience in the field. She wanted to be sure that a practical, on-the-ground perspective ran throughout the work ahead. Steve's participation provided further support from the top as the commissioner and her team sought to challenge the status quo way of doing things.

Engaging with a key partner: SEIU Local 509

Late in August, two weeks after the news of two-year-old Avalena's death, the steering committee met for the first time in a small conference room in the department's downtown Boston office. The Child Welfare League of America paper and other reports had established a fact base. The investigations underway would provide critical additional information. Now it was time to translate the facts into what the department needed to do.

Steve conducted a round-the-table discussion (see chapter 2), starting with the commissioner. Linda began by pointing out that the recent tragedies were examples of the stresses on the system. She emphasized that without significant changes at the department, more such incidents might occur at any time. The others in attendance followed with their concerns. They noted an overall lack of capacity in both management and staff, unclear protocols and practices, and weak communications within the department and with its partners. Together, they described just how long it took to do anything, from developing policy to hiring staffers. At the close of the meeting, two hours later, we had a beginning framework for what to do.

While the team was beginning the work to turn around the agency, I was preparing to take on my role as the public face of what had happened and what we were doing. On September 4, the DCF announced the findings from the investigation of the Jack Loiselle case. The report was blunt and clear: Not only had the department failed to protect this seven-year-old boy, who was beaten and starved by his father, but it had failed to pull together multiple reports of abuse. The investigation chronicled a long list of meetings that department social workers and others had had with little Jack on a regular basis. The staff seemed to have acted according to protocols, but the department had looked at each instance of abuse and concern separately, not at what they all meant together.

At a press conference, I emphasized what we planned to do: develop policies to address current gaps and provide staff training so that social workers on the ground and their managers understood how best to implement these changes.

Behind the scenes, I met with Secretary Sudders, Commissioner Spears, and the department's top union officials from SEIU Local 509, who represented the department's social workers. We quickly reached a common understanding of the need for more staffing, better technology, and improved clinical support. But I also wanted to concentrate on the critical policy gaps identified in the league report and by the department's recent investigations. Any change in policy was required to be "negotiated" with the union; some blamed this requirement for how long it took to develop department policies. I wanted everyone at the meeting to understand how foundational these operational policies were, how important it was that the people who would be carrying them out—the social workers and supervisors (aka SEIU members)—be involved in their development, and how quickly the new policies must be implemented. When the SEIU leads agreed, it was a BFD (big frigging deal)—one small step for the process, one giant leap for fast-tracking department policy development.

Structuring the Turnaround

With the leaders and the team in place and following the facts giving us a foundation for what to do, the effort would move to the focus on how. The department's approach to how to do it had three distinct elements.

First, Commissioner Spears established the Agency Improvement Leadership Team. Its name didn't exactly roll off the tongue, but each word was deliberately chosen. "Agency" referred to the entire department, but also to the ability to perform. "Improvement" signaled that this effort would be about step-by-step progress—not a leap to one solution but a steady recovery and advance. "Leadership" referred to both the involvement of key department directors and managers and the action of leading. And "Team" defined the approach as *we*, not the commissioner alone or a handful of others but the full group.

The team would meet two times a week for several hours. It was made up of two dozen leaders from the central and field offices, including the steering committee. This wouldn't be a matter of the central office dictating to the field, a phenomenon that is frequently heard about and rightly criticized. By including all the regional directors from across the state, Linda emphasized that this turnaround effort involved the department team as a whole. She also underscored how important it was that the field staff have a strong voice in every aspect of the change process—from discovery and development to decision-making and delivery. She understood that the DCF's services would be delivered from its twenty-nine area offices. How those offices performed would be the ultimate measure of results.

Second, the turnaround initiative was broken down into work streams. The commissioner named five areas of accountability: *Policy and practice* would center on new policies and protocols and the training and support for better practice. *People* would focus on identifying and filling gaps in the staff, including social workers, managers, and medical professionals. *Management structure* would ensure that the organizational structure and roles and responsibilities—from social workers on up through supervisors, managers, and directors—were robust enough to support this difficult work. *Metrics and reporting* would provide detailed accountability for performance and the tracking of progress on improvement efforts. Finally, *communications* would have both an internal agency focus and a mandate to keep the wide network of outside partners informed.

Each work stream would be led by two cochairs, one from the central office and the other from the field, to ensure a direct connection between the intent of policy and the realities of implementation. Working with their teams, the cochairs would be responsible for defining, planning, and implementing their work plan with support from the project management team.

Third, improvements would be released on a regular basis. The idea was to leverage a release date in determining what to do within a particular time frame. As we have noted, emphasizing time in the project-planning triangle (see chapter 3) of time, resources, and scope drives urgency. Further, the short time frame—release windows of eight to ten weeks—directly challenged the status quo way of doing business. The department could not tolerate a wait of up to eighteen months, as it had in the past, for the development and rollout of a new policy. It could not wait the many months it typically took to make a single hire. The release concept demanded a new approach and, as any significant change required union support, we needed the SEIU's leadership backing.

The release concept provided the department with the discipline needed to prioritize. It forced decision-making. It made tangible getting things done fast. Using the concept, Linda Spears could be clear about the current focus and the following steps. The organization breathed a collective sigh of relief. Items not addressed would not be forgotten. They would be scheduled for release as appropriate. With a focus on fewer things at any one time, not only were concrete results realized in a matter of weeks, but more was accomplished sooner and at a higher quality. The release approach combined the principle of project prioritization with the project-planning physics of managing time, scope, and resources.

Plan the Work, Work the Plan

On Wednesday, September 16, 2015, two weeks after the first steering committee meeting, Spears convened the Agency Improvement Leadership Team. The meeting was held in a long, rectangular conference room with several tables laid end to end. A second row of chairs ringed the room. It was a tight space with low ceilings and no windows. More than twenty department leaders and the project management staff filled the seats.

Linda began by thanking the group for the work they were doing every day. She discussed the urgency of the improvements required. She acknowledged that the need for improvement in the department wasn't new, but together we would try a new way to achieve it. Business as usual just wouldn't do. Then she asked them all to introduce themselves and answer one question: "What are the impediments to success?"

So the first leadership team meeting began with round-the-table participation. Unlike many, if not most, meetings, where lots of people attend and sit by quietly while someone makes a presentation, the round-the-table technique ensures that everyone participates. Each person's voice is heard. Every member engages from the outset.

Everyone in the room dove right in. The responses flowed. How can we quickly develop the policies needed while also ensuring appropriate input? We're short-staffed now, and we take forever to hire; how can we fill the current gaps, never mind all the spots needed? We need to improve how we implement policies and protocols in the field, which are applied inconsistently from office to office. Can the technology system handle the changes needed? Do we have a management structure that makes sense, not just one that matches the funds available?

After this opening discussion, Linda shifted gears and moved from impediments to how to do it. She said that DCF would continue with an overall focus on the best interests of the children. She outlined the five initial areas of accountability. She announced the work-stream cochairs—a central office person and a field person for each—and said that a dedicated project management team was ready to provide support. She confirmed that everyone would be trained in and expected to use the agile scrum methodology. We believed that it could be used to good effect here. In closing, she noted that the first release date was in November. She expected that at the next meeting, each work-stream group would be prepared to present an outline of what it would get done in the coming ten weeks.

Steve attended the steering committee and leadership team meetings, and in our one-to-one morning calls, he updated me on the department's efforts. Next, he and I would focus on the immediate problems to solve. Who would be lined up to provide legal, HR, and other staff resources? What were the considerations for additional funds? When was it best to update the legislative leadership? I was able to stay informed, provide guidance, and break down some barriers within the bureaucracy, whether real or perceived.

Two days later, on Friday, September 18, the leadership team met for a second time. Each of the five work streams was to report on its progress and issues. The people team went first. It reported that 160 new positions would be posted over the next two weeks. With support from the governor's office, additional help was secured from the state's human resources division. A review was underway to consider how to streamline the hiring process.

Policy and practice came next. Its first focus would be on policies relating to intake and supervision. These critical but outdated policies had been called out in the league report and highlighted in the Loiselle investigation. *Intake* describes the initial notification of a potential case and the information surrounding it. This policy provides structure for evaluating a situation and what actions may be necessary, ranging from immediate emergency intervention to seeking more information. *Supervision* describes the day-to-day efforts of the social worker and others in the department to monitor and support the child. Although there were a number of big gaps in operational policies, the proposal to tackle those two items first made sense. Intake and supervision created a foundation for much of the department's work. It was noted that eight people would staff the policy and practice team, not just the one or two who had typically been involved. The commissioner also outlined the union's involvement and the SEIU's commitment to support an expedited process. She emphasized that this work had to be completed in a couple of months, not the year-plus it might ordinarily take.

The other work streams followed. Communications discussed its development of a comprehensive plan for both internal and external audiences. The management structure team noted that it was evaluating how to reestablish a regional management office that had been lost to funding reductions by the previous administration. Metrics and reporting reviewed some initial ideas about key performance metrics and the frequency of reporting.

The meeting ended with a round-the-table discussion. This time it was open ended. Any participant could make an observation, raise a concern, request help, or ask a question. A few commented skeptically about the feasibility of hiring so quickly. Someone noted how critical it was to involve the union and others in the policy development process. Several asked about the timing and content of upcoming communications items.

Her name was Bella

At just about the time the leadership meeting convened, we learned about the terrible circumstances of Baby Doe, now identified as Bella. Suffolk County District Attorney Daniel Conley held a press conference describing what they had learned. The DA's office had received a tip the previous day; the body had been identified and the alleged murderers arrested. The child's name was Bella. She was about two and a half years old when she died. The circumstances were gruesome. Bella's mother and her boyfriend were being held for committing the crime. The announcement ended several months of investigations that had followed tips from around the world. The DCF reported that it had not had an open case with this family for more than two years but had had brief involvement with Baby Bella as an infant.

I'm a dad. With two sons and a daughter. I kept thinking of the horrors inflicted upon that little girl. In a moment alone, I wiped away my tears. It was simply crushing.

Our work seemed ever more urgent. I walked into Steve's office later that day and he had clipped the picture of Bella and put it on the wall next to his desk. Her picture was at eye level just a few feet away. I knew the point he was making without asking and couldn't have agreed more. For everyone who came into his office, starting with cabinet members, agency heads, and well-heeled lobbyists, this was about the importance of the work that we do, especially for those whose voices are not heard.

Persistence and progress

The following Monday, September 21, the leadership team met for the third time in five days. Linda opened the meeting by acknowledging Bella's case and the pain felt throughout the agency. The atmosphere was somber and reflective. She asked that anyone who wished to speak do so.

In the most difficult circumstances, the leadership and teams are tested. At such times, I think about the quality of persistence—the strength to keep driving forward. At this critical moment, Linda and her team were demonstrating the persistence they would need for the long haul ahead.

Quick progress highlights from several of the work streams followed, with two updates from the management structure team. The first centered on restaffing the regional office that had been eliminated by budget cuts after the Great Recession. The western and central regions had been combined to encompass about half the state, so the current western region included all the cities and towns from Worcester west to the New York border. That was enormous not just geographically, but also in the number of cases for which it was responsible. It accounted for 48 percent of the entire department caseload. Now the team proposed keeping the existing western regional office management structure and adding back the central regional office, with six new management positions, to bring back needed organizational support and supervision.

The second update concerned management at each of the department's twenty-nine area offices. Budget cuts had torn at the structure of those offices as well. While the regional offices provided essential top-level supervision and cogent problem-solving support, the area offices remained the hub of ongoing case activity. To save funds, the previous administration had sliced some of their management teams in half, leaving a full team for every two offices. The process was referred to as "coupling." The team noted that plans were underway to "decouple" the merged teams and reinstate full leadership at each area office.

Addressing the regional office and area office management structure resolved two significant problems raised by the Child Welfare League of America report. And it gave the leadership team a sense of agency. Its members felt empowered to perform.

The leadership team would meet again that week and then several times a week as it focused on the progress of the five work streams. The agile scrum methodology accelerated their work. The project management team provided hands-on support. Commissioner Spears engaged the steering committee to resolve cross-team and cross-agency issues. All in all, relentless, persistent progress.

Revamping hiring

The DCF needed more managers and staffers. Not just a few, but hundreds. When it comes to adding staff members, funding is always an issue. But to everyone's credit, from the governor's budget team to the legislature, that was readily addressed. Now the department had to make it happen.

We understand that some differences between the private and public sectors can exacerbate the time it takes to hire. Legal requirements and protocols in the public sector exist for a reason and should be respected. However, employment practices in public-sector agencies are often not just risk-averse but silted up with leftover habits, arcane procedures, and non-value-added reviews. Slow hiring can mean no hiring as potential candidates make other choices. And slow hiring hurts an agency's performance when it lacks the personnel to deliver expected services, even if it has the budget to do so.

For an agency that had been taking months to make a single hire, the magnitude of the call for rapid hiring was beyond daunting. The DCF could not afford to do things in the same way and get the same results.

With staff members from the governor's Strategic Ops Team in the lead, we proposed a business-process-analysis approach to redo the agency's employment methods. This method lays out the details of every step in a process from beginning to end and then tears it apart—eliminating redundancy, busting through bottlenecks, junking irrelevant steps—to create a simpler, streamlined process.

In short order, a team analyzed the department's hiring process, scrutinizing how it worked from recruitment to the first day on the job. The review found a lengthy process with much time between steps, limited initial recruitment efforts that relied heavily on what was politely called the post-and-hope tactic, dated practices for interviewing, and more than a dozen approvals required for a single hire. It was clear why filling a single position could take months.

The team then developed a new process that dropped unnecessary steps, prescribed shorter time frames for key actions, and performed some tasks simultaneously rather than sequentially. A full package of new outreach and recruitment activities filled an important gap. A tracking system measured key metrics, from the date of the job posting to the winning candidate's first day on the job. Taking a page from the private sector, one innovation brought it all together: job fairs. Not exactly a groundbreaking concept. But a job fair, with its robust advertising and multiple same-day interviews, could produce dozens of hires in a single day. So positive were the results of the first one that regions across the state copied it immediately and competed to get the best results.

In less than a year, hundreds of new caseworkers had been hired, dozens were added to the medical clinical team, and new management positions were filled in the local area offices and at department headquarters.

The DCF met its first release goals in November 2015 and its second release goals in March 2016. Further releases followed. It was engaged in a step-by-step transformation. Together, Linda Spears and the leadership team learned not just how important the concept of the release was to successful implementation, but also how critical release planning was. They built it in as a key task for each work stream.

As each release was coming to an end, planning would start for the next one. Each work stream presented its expected accomplishments for the upcoming release at a leadership team meeting. This allowed for a joint review of proposed tasks and also revealed key interdependencies between the work streams. Typically, a team's vision of what could be completed within the short release time frame was grander than what was possible. Ambition was encouraged because it created a stretch that might not otherwise have occurred and gave a head start on the next release. Nevertheless, focus was important. As each team began its work, Linda led a discussion about what should be

A Big Item for the Fix-It Toolkit

Tips Tools and Tactics

We like to make something work better than it did before. When we focus on the delivery of services, whether it's internal to the organization or a public program, fixing things usually means going deep into how things work. The review of the detailed steps where things are taken apart and then put back together—only better—serves as a big tool in our fix-it toolkit. It's called "business-process analysis" and comes directly from the private sector, but its application is every bit as effective in the public sector.

Business-process analysis is a simple discipline that focuses on, say, a lengthy hiring process, an unwieldy application process, or a faulty data process. It makes such processes work better and faster with less time and expense.

In reviewing how the work is getting done, the team must first ask: Is this working? Is this what we want the customer experience to be? Then it moves from *pointing out a problem* to *problem-solving*. The team must ask: How do we make this better? Why is this step necessary? What if we did it this way? It will take a few sessions to scrutinize the existing process and then develop options for improving, streamlining, or completely redesigning how work is done.

If you or your team has not done this before, consider bringing in someone within your organization or a consultant who has. While it is not difficult to do, especially for the first time, having the experienced guide can be a big help in being objective and efficient.

Ready? Here are the steps:

1. **Ditch the org chart.** Convene people who understand and perform all aspects of the process, including technology systems. (While their bosses may want to participate, the folks that actually know how things work need to be in the room.)

2. **Determine the as-is state—how things are working today.** Determine the beginning and end of the process and chart the following: (a) How exactly is this activity is being performed? (b) How do the activities move from one step of the process to the next (i.e., what's paper, digital, phone, etc.)? (c) Who exactly is doing what at each step? (d) What are the handoffs between individuals, teams, and systems?

3. **Convene a second session to focus on the to-be state.** Ask: How can we make the process work faster, simpler, and, if possible, save money? Are there redundant process loops, unnecessary approvals, and slow or broken transitions between steps? Look at what we can drop, modify, and clean up.

4. **Document the potential improvements.** You have described the current state and what the future process could look like. Now capture the specific improvements, the anticipated performance results—time saved, faster processing, budget savings, and on. Identify what it will take to implement.

5. **Communicate with all involved parties.** As you develop the implementation plan, let folks know the overall timing, how the changes will be supported, including any new training needed.

6. **Measure results.** Celebrate the improvement, and always be ready to make adjustments.

prioritized and what could be dropped or deferred. It was the discipline of making scope choices while adhering to deadlines.

The caseload conundrum

As planning for the third release was underway, the department was showing solid overall improvement. However, the average caseload for social workers remained troubling. As at so many other human services agencies, the work at the DCF is all about one-to-one interactions between social workers and clients—the children and adults involved. This intense work draws on a social worker's training, knowledge, skills, and experience. Each case requires personal engagement at the child's home. Heavy caseloads threatened the ability to provide the care and attention needed.

At the beginning of the turnaround, the department reported that the average caseload for social workers was nineteen, whereas fifteen was the target. Not bad on paper, so why did it feel so much worse to the staff, managers, families, and service partners? It was an example of why we hate averages. The average masked what was happening with individual staff members and at the area offices.

We had followed the facts, but they were not the right ones to get at this core problem. If we continued to use the average as the key metric result, there would be some improvement, but potentially not where it was most needed. The elements of the Results Framework—people, facts, how, results—were in place, but unless a significant adjustment was made, the imbalance in individual social worker's caseloads could endanger vulnerable children and families.

As the second release was reaching completion, I asked for a meeting to discuss what would come next. The changes in policy, infrastructure, and staffing achieved in the previous few months were impressive and critical to any sustained progress. Yet I wanted to understand what was going on in the DCF's twenty-nine local offices and with the individual caseworkers. I wanted to know how many social workers had heavy caseloads, which offices were performing well, and which offices needed help. I believed that learning these results and providing feedback for how the programs were implemented were critical to ultimately improving the experience of the children and families served by DCF.

Self-Reinforcing Momentum

Just as the circumstances of each child are unique, so is each case. Caseworkers are expected to handle it all, and time and time again, they do so successfully. But if a caseworker is overwhelmed, or unclear about what to do, or in need of other resources and support, the consequences can literally be life-threatening. The caseload ratio, while not the only measure, was meant to demonstrate how many children a social worker could safely serve. Achieving the target ratio was more than a technical, numeric goal. At the end of the day, the purpose was profoundly human—to provide services in support of the most vulnerable children.

After focusing on the foundational work of improving operational policies and increasing organizational capacity, the third release, launched in April 2016, was aimed at better managing caseloads. And while the earlier releases had targeted department-wide problems, the third focused on the twenty-nine local offices. They were the base of operations for individual social workers, providing supervision, clerical support, and other resources. A data review supported the premise that caseloads varied not only by individual, but also by area office. A small number of the offices had staffing and case counts that were fairly reasonably balanced. But most did not.

This initiative was designed to free social workers to pay more attention to each child and their family. Data analytics drove the approach. The details for individual social workers revealed significant discrepancies, with some carrying fewer than fifteen cases, but more than 40 percent responsible for twenty or more. Additional facts for each field office, including each social worker's years of experience and the status of each case, helped in assessing performance. On the basis of the data, each office was assigned to one of five categories, from high performing to needing significant intervention. Each regional director then established a team made up of local office and central office staffers to develop and execute caseload-management strategy plans that were specific to the local office, as well as to the individual needs of the social worker.

A top priority for reducing the caseload ratio was adding more social workers and support staffers. As the former were hired and trained, they were immediately added to the number of active caseworkers. A newly created position, social worker technician, could take on some tasks, and additional administrative staffers took over some time-consuming clerical activities that had previously been borne by the caseworkers.

Although the added staff delivered much-needed help, a typical social worker faced other challenges. Some found themselves spending lots of time arranging for transportation or using their own vehicles and time to get children to medical and other appointments. The DCF responded with new transportation resources to help the families directly and thereby free up staff time. The department also found additional safe childcare places so that caregivers could go to work or counseling appointments—and the social workers didn't have to fill a void with on-the-spot childcare. Further, new clinical staff members were dispersed throughout the regional and local offices to address the need for timely access to medical and other clinical advice. And an increase in management positions in certain offices helped social workers better handle their cases.

During this time, the full leadership team regularly did a deep dive into progress and problems at the local offices. A regional director would present the status of the work in each of the offices in their jurisdiction, backed up by detailed performance metrics.

The regional directors' presentations and the discussion that followed were great examples of measure, evaluate, adjust, repeat. A presentation would begin with key baseline statistics on staffing and cases and then go on to describe performance outliers—both good and bad—and what specific problems individual social workers and local offices were encountering. The director would outline the specific interventions implemented, including access to new childcare vouchers and approved overtime for additional case reviews. The directors were frank about what worked and where concepts still needed help to be practically implemented. Their colleagues jumped right in with questions, advice, and comments. No detail was too small if it was thought to make a difference. The next time a director presented, we could all see the new measurements resulting from the adjustments made. The sense of achievement was palpable. This focus on the details provided self-reinforcing momentum—relentless progress.

The work launched in the third release proved successful and continued, along with other improvements, in the releases to follow. By August 2017, the results were a meaningful reduction in individual caseloads and improved performance across the offices. The number of social workers responsible for more than twenty-three families each dropped from 187 to 9. For those with twenty to twenty-two families, the number was reduced from 455 to 155. The median number of families per social worker dropped from nineteen to sixteen. Overall, the share of social workers with twenty or more cases dropped from

42 percent to 11 percent. There was still plenty to do. But the progress to protect vulnerable children and families was significant.

The evaluation by office and by caseworker had informed how best to provide the support needed. The status quo view of the data in terms of averages had concealed performance realities. Not until the data had been unpacked at the level of the individual experience were the most effective interventions made.

Still More to Be Done

Over the years, Steve and I would observe that significant progress on a major organizational turnaround takes three years. A lot is accomplished in the first couple of years, but in our experience, it's not until the third year that the organization shows its sustained new capacity and capabilities.

In January 2018, several months into the third year of the DCF turnaround, Secretary Sudders and Commissioner Spears provided an overall progress report to the lieutenant governor and me at one of our regular update meetings. A snapshot from September 2015 to December 2017 captured the transformation underway since the turnaround had begun.

Among the achievements to note:

- Key policy gaps had been filled, including intake, supervision, case closing, and children missing from care. For some policies, this was the first major update in decades.

- More than 280 new social workers were on staff. The department had gone from 54 percent to nearly 99 percent of licensed social workers, the highest percentage of licensed and trained staffers ever.

- The medical clinical support team quadrupled from eight people to include a full-time medical director for the first time, a child psychiatry consultant, six nurses, and twenty-nine medical social workers.

- Regional and area office management structures had been reestablished. The department built vital management capacity by adding a sixth regional office, breaking up a single area that encompassed half the state and half the caseload while supplementing supervisory and management staff at the twenty-nine local offices.

- Leaping from the 1980s to the present, laptops were provided to social workers so that they could access important information on the spot without having to go into the office.

- Caseloads per social worker were the lowest in more than a decade.

Since the DCF turnaround began, Spears and her team have continued to work to provide child safety and family support services and tackle yet-unaddressed problems. The improvements made in policy, staffing, caseloads, management structure, clinical support, and other services have been sustained and continue to get stronger. While there remains work to do, improving foster care placements, expanding adoption opportunities, and additional reporting have also been addressed in the past few years.

Nevertheless, the death of fourteen-year-old David Almond, in October 2020, showed how much there remains to be done. David, a teen with disabilities, was abused and starved in his father's home. In March 2021, an investigation by the Office of the Child Advocate found widespread systemic failure to protect this child, including by the Fall River School Department and the DCF. David had been living in a group home and attending a special-needs school, but despite the urging of those providers to delay the return of David to his family and a court judgment that his father was unfit for parenting, the department had David join his father and other adults and children in a small apartment.

In a virtual briefing with reporters to discuss the child advocate's investigation, Secretary Sudders and Commissioner Spears conceded that the "safety net failed." Spears added, "The circumstances in this case are inexplicable to me. There's no rationale that accounts for the decision to reunify these children given their risks and concerns for this family."[3] Two department managers were fired, and one retired before being terminated.

We recognize that this tragedy happened during the Covid-19 epidemic, which tested all aspects of the agency. Still, it shows that the Results Framework is not foolproof. Actions, including site visits and coordination among involved parties, that were expected to happen did not, exposing vulnerabilities in policy and adherence to protocols.

David Almond's death exposed the lack of appropriate department policy and practice regarding children with disabilities. The Baker-Polito administration has embraced the recommendations of the child advocate as a road map for addressing these problems. At a press conference following the release of the report, I said, "I expect and anticipate that everything in there is going to be implemented, and it's going to be implemented on a statewide basis, and it's going to get implemented as fast as it possibly can be."[4]

A legislative hearing in May 2021 probed further into the child advocate's investigation and the DCF's actions. As the *Boston Globe* reported, "That DCF is again facing similar questions, however, is not a reflection of the progress it has made but rather the ever-evolving challenges in keeping 40,000-plus risk-children safe, according to other child advocates."[5] The *Globe* went on to quote Mary A. McGeown, the executive director of Massachusetts Society for the Prevention of Cruelty to Children. She pointed out that unlike after other earlier tragedies, DCF has made serious efforts to improve over the last six years, including increasing the number of adoptions and adding new specialized workers. McGeown added, "If I could change this one thing, I think we should stop referring to it as 'reforming' the department. That suggests there's going to be an end. Our child welfare system needs to be continually enhanced."

. . .

We tell this story to demonstrate that the principles and approach of the Results Framework can work in settings as complicated as the Department of Children and Families, where every single case is unique and the consequences of weak performance are profound. This story highlights the key features of people are policy, with new leadership tapping into the skills and experience of current staffers. It also demonstrates that a focus on people alone is not enough. The comprehensive approach of the Results Framework is needed. The project management team is a key engine for change, through its training, support, facilitation, and work products. A tech-based project management process like agile scrum can be implemented in a culture not of engineers but of social workers—who were as open to new tools and methods as any group we have seen. This story also shows the immense possibilities of a business process analysis and the breakthroughs that can occur when averages are deconstructed into individual experiences.

We tell this story because it illustrates how the Results Framework provided a platform to do more, faster, not only to address one-off issues, but to realize sustainable outcomes. Much has been accomplished. New challenges have emerged and will continue to do so. We believe that the DCF, as a result of the framework, is positioned to actively address problems, make important changes quickly, and build forward. For our most vulnerable children, the imperative is relentless improvement.

Managing through a Pandemic

Covid-19

I n 2020 and 2021, we all lived through a national and global tragedy—and high public-sector drama. As we write in the late fall of 2021, some twenty months after what was at first quaintly called the novel coronavirus, it is certainly clear that the virus will continue to be with us for the foreseeable future. The impact of Covid-19 on jobs, schools, housing, and health care—with the widespread illness and loss of life—has been acute and scarring. In Massachusetts, and in government generally, we were not prepared for a global pandemic.

Since the beginning of my administration, we had been formally and informally addressing both natural and manmade crises using the Results Framework. Then came Covid. Intuitively, I saw it as a crisis that would unfold in stages—but the nature and length of each stage was unknowable. As the months have passed, this historic event has seemed like a fight in three acts: the scramble, the struggle to reopen, and the race to vaccinate. All along the way, we leaned into the principles of the framework again and again.

The Scramble (March 2020–May 2020)

The first stage of the pandemic was a rapid-fire collection of actions and reactions at hyper-speed. Here was a national crisis—in fact, an international scourge—and confusion reigned. Limited, conflicting data was followed by vacillating federal guidance regarding masks, the virus, and how best to fight it.

With the federal government effectively punting on what to do—except, to its credit, initiating Operation Warp Speed to develop vaccines—each state was on its own. True, Covid hit hardest and earliest on the coasts and may not have been viewed as a national catastrophe from day one. Nevertheless, the Food and Drug Administration (FDA), Centers for Disease Control and Prevention (CDC), and the power of the purse are centered in the nation's capital, and many states were looking to the feds for leadership. There was a lot of politics but not much policy, and even less guidance on implementing the scant protocols and processes that might work. The scramble was on.

The sixty-plus days after the beginning of March were a scramble in every possible way—to sort out reliable information, to try to contain the crisis, and to communicate accurately, nimbly, and frequently. Like other Northeastern states, Massachusetts faced some specific challenges. We have the third-highest population density in the country (behind New Jersey and Rhode Island). We have cold winters, an older population, and older building infrastructure, and we spend more time indoors. We got hit hard by Covid-19 early.

From the beginning, the overarching objective was to protect the public health in order to ensure that we had hospital and health system capacity to meet the unprecedented demand many were forecasting. We worked 24/7 to build up public health capacity, reduce business activity and public gatherings, and prepare to safely reopen when it was possible to do so. And we had to do all three at once. No one knew what was ahead, but we knew we needed to create the infrastructure for an extended emergency response.

Top-tier team

When addressing a problem, it's people are policy first. This means selecting the leadership and building the team to ensure knowledge, know-how, and capacity. It means identifying what's needed and then appointing the very best individuals for the task at hand. People are policy acknowledges the primacy of the selection of people as part of policy development; people will address the problem and bring these concepts to fruition. Getting this right would set up everything that would follow.

I conferred with my closest advisers, Lieutenant Governor Karyn Polito, senior adviser Tim Buckley, and Chief of Staff Kristen Lepore (Steve had left his position a few years earlier for an academic fellowship). What might this team look like and who should lead it? Tim had been our campaign communications lead and communications director for the governor's office before he was selected for this role. Kristen had been the secretary of administration and finance at the onset of my term. She and I had met some twenty years before, when I was Governor Weld's secretary of administration and finance, and she was a budget analyst.

While the extent of the emergency was not clear, what we knew about it compelled strong action: a dedicated team with a direct report to me. The Covid-19 Response Command Center would provide the hyper-focus required. Picking someone to lead this effort was shaping up to be among the most important decisions I would face as governor.

In Massachusetts, we're blessed with world-class hospitals, medical research facilities, and public health leaders. We have a vast talent pool for this type of assignment. I would need it. For the leader of the Covid-19 Command Center, I needed someone who understood those worlds and was respected in them but knew how to get things done in this complex ecosystem where the public and private sectors collided. I chose my secretary of health and human services. Marylou Sudders is a social worker. A fighter with a hard exterior and a compassionate core. Marylou knows how to speedily move from program concept to implementation. And she's willing to change course if the facts so indicate. When the going got tough, she was the one I wanted in the foxhole. She would never quit.

Marylou would retain her place in the cabinet but take a leave to dedicate herself fully to the Covid-19 emergency. Her first task would be to build out the structure and team of the Covid-19 Command Center—fast. Forty-eight hours later, the command center was operational.

As point person on Covid, Marylou would work closely with Kristen. The command center personnel included talent borrowed from several state agencies and private organizations. These were people who knew their way around public health, health care, and state and local government. Consultants provided heavy-duty analytics and project-management support. The Department of Public Health, led by Commissioner Monica Bharel, provided expertise in collaborating with the command center and our state agencies. For other support, I asked Steve to be available to Marylou and to me for consultation on this and other assignments.

In creating the command center, I was following a key principle of the framework—not only establishing a central point of coordination, but also envisioning the right form of governance and an effective decision-making process. I expected the command center to digest incoming information, provide regular public reporting, manage our efforts to fight the virus, and measure the success of the efforts, all while working with multiple state and local agencies as well as the health-care community. I insisted that Marylou and Kristen be in open and constant contact. It was imperative that they each know what the other was working on, and be able to close gaps in communications and follow through. During this time, my office held daily virtual meetings with Marylou at the command center, establishing a practical forum for both information sharing and fast decision-making.

Facing the facts

Again, following the framework, I insisted that the Covid response take a fact-based approach. We needed to gather scientific and medical data, gauge the on-the-ground impact of the coronavirus on our residents, and watch what others were doing around the nation and the world. But news and advice about the virus was changing constantly, so we needed more help. Who had to wear a mask? When? Where? Should tests be reserved for people with flu-like symptoms? Were people contagious only when they showed symptoms? To provide guidance on these and hundreds of other questions that followed, I asked that a group of experts—the Covid-19 Medical Advisory Board—be established to provide us with insight.

The board met virtually for the first time on March 19, 2020. It included medical leaders, infectious disease specialists, and researchers from the deep well of talent that already worked in the

Commonwealth. It meet weekly, online—with Marylou, Kristen, Tim, Karyn, Monica Bharel, and me—to discuss policies, federal pronouncements, and competing narratives about Covid-19 that were appearing in various medical journals. Especially during the first months of our Covid-19 response, their collective wisdom provided invaluable guidance. And as the medical evidence or the facts on the ground changed, the command center team and the board quickly synthesized new information and discussed how to adjust.

By the end of March, I had issued more than twenty Covid-19 orders, exceeding the total number of emergency orders I had made during the previous five-plus years of my administration. They constricted almost all discretionary public activities—imposing limits on gatherings, restricting how businesses could operate, closing public schools, and stopping visitation to long-term-care facilities. Effectively, we threw an enormous wrench into life as we knew it.

Those measures stunned many people. Some called them an overreaction, especially since there was no guarantee that the federal government would step up to assist everyone hard-hit by these orders. But given how little we knew about Covid-19, the lack of easily available testing, the scarcity of personal protective equipment (PPE), and the mysteries of how to operate safely in this environment, we had little choice. Protecting the health of the public was our primary mission at that point in time, and these were the measures that were available to us.

I emphasized starting with the first two steps of the framework— people and facts—because too often these seemingly obvious elements are overlooked. When decision makers jump to declare a solution, the problem may remain unresolved. An *announcement* is not the same as a *result*. Starting with a robust team ensures that we have the capacity to oversee a crisis and the know-how to drive results. We require the team to dive into the facts. It's imperative to see the data evidence—in this case, how people contracted the virus, what research was telling us about effectively preventing transmission, and how to care for people when they got sick. Further, we need to understand the points of pain for real people—illness, lost jobs, the threat of eviction or foreclosure, and shortages of food and utilities. Finally, the team needs to learn how others have tackled similar circumstances.

Once we've gathered relevant facts, the focus shifts to *what* to do to solve the problem and *how* to do it. This is granular work: defining the specific action needed and establishing the ability to carry it through. Right from the beginning, it was clear that testing and acquiring PPE would be gargantuan challenges. We focused on how to resolve these and the other issues that kept emerging.

For all this work, we insisted on metrics to measure results. Overall metrics such as total case counts and hospitalizations provided critical information about the battle with Covid-19. Specific measures such as infection rates in nursing homes and the extent of contact tracing told us whether our approach was working. A rigorous review of results illuminates what needs to change because it's not working and what needs to be accelerated because it is. Sustained, creative effort is vital; metrics are the objective measure of performance.

These steps seem simple, but they require an intense attention to detail, a specific implementation plan, and the humility to readily make course corrections. They provided the structure for the work ahead.

Necessity is the mother of invention

The chaotic chase for PPE gave us the first inkling that Covid would be unlike anything we'd seen before. Here we were, literally competing with other states and the feds for masks, gloves, and gowns, because nobody had enough PPE—not in storage, not in inventory, not even in production. I was hopeful that we would soon receive 3 million masks, which we were expecting from a local retailer, but they were literally stolen at the Port of New York when the federal government impounded the shipment.

In March, with the number of cases beginning to soar, the state lacked the PPE for those who needed it most. The problem to solve was flashing red. A focus on how led us to decide to become our own global procurement agency. After many false starts and hundreds of phone calls, we found someone who could access masks in China. But we still had to get them to Massachusetts without being seized by the federal government. For that I needed a very big private plane. I reached out to the Kraft family, owners of the New England Patriots, to ask if they would donate their plane and pilots to the cause. They agreed immediately. I then called Alaska Governor Mike Dunleavy and asked if we could route the flight to China through his state. He agreed, and his team kept a watchful eye on our cargo as the plane was refueled and inspected on its return trip from China.

At the end of March, with no public announcement, the Patriots plane took off from Rhode Island and landed in Anchorage. The crew took care of paperwork, followed rest guidelines, and then flew to Shenzhen, the fifth-largest city in China. At the Shenzhen airport, as required, no one got off and no one got on. The gear was loaded into the plane, and in just under three hours on the ground (the prescribed time limit), the plane headed back to Alaska. It landed at Boston's Logan Airport on April 2, where it was met on the tarmac by the Massachusetts State Police and National Guard. I was taking no chances.

At the airport press conference, I got emotional when expressing my gratitude to the Kraft family and especially to Jonathan Kraft. Nurses, home health workers, long-term-care staffers, and first responders had all been telling me their concerns about contracting Covid because they lacked adequate PPE. They were less worried about themselves than about spreading the illness to a parent, a grandparent, or a patient. Their constant selfless acts made me deeply grateful that finally—*finally*—we had some gear to help.

That successful mission was a model for six more charter flights over the next couple of months. Millions of masks, gowns, swabs, and other assorted PPE made their way to our health-care facilities, nursing homes, and workers on the front line.

At the same time, I wanted to engage local manufacturers (something the feds could have done but didn't seem interested in doing) to build a domestic PPE pipeline. Through an innovative program using state funds to support the revamping of their facilities, we partnered with Massachusetts businesses to produce masks, gowns, coveralls, gloves, and other gear. This was one of the only state programs of its kind in the country, and in a matter of weeks and months, manufacturers were producing and distributing millions of federally approved PPE for thousands of workers.

The focus on how, the relentless persistence, the creativity—all allowed us to start filling the PPE gap.

Testing and tracing—the need for speed

While we were chasing PPE, we also had to expand our testing capacity. One of my first assignments for Marylou and the command center was to do that, with or without the support of the CDC. The virus was unquestionably here, and it was clearly contagious. Only adequate testing would tell us who was being affected and in what communities, and help us understand and address Covid transmission. Marylou called together a dedicated team at the command center to work on all things testing.

By the end of March, Massachusetts was administering 1,500 tests a day. But many of the tests being processed were days or even weeks old, well beyond the most infectious time period. Too many people with symptoms could not get a test, never mind the folks they were in contact with. Community transmission raged on until this first public health step was in place.

The testing team reviewed results daily from more than a hundred entities, revealing problems to address (data gaps, inconsistent reporting, technology glitches) and where to leverage strong performance. Changes were rushed to increase speed and capacity, week over week. By the end of April, the number of Covid tests had grown to 8,500 a day. This precept of the Results Framework—measure, evaluate, adjust, repeat—paid off. With steady improvement underway, the team turned to increasing testing another tenfold.

I always try to reach outside my office for information. My discussions with infectious disease experts convinced me that we had to have a robust statewide contact-tracing program if we were to contain the spread of the virus. Few other states were then talking about such a statewide program. But Covid was still a mystery to most of us, and anything we could do to help those who came down with it—staying isolated and safe while they were contagious—would reduce the spread. The same applied to their close contacts.

We had a problem to solve. I knew that local boards of health could do some of this work, but their capacity varied from community to community, and if case numbers grew quickly, they could be overwhelmed. What to do? We created the Community Tracing Collaborative to support local health boards (see chapter 3). It linked Partners In Health, a Boston-based global organization that had done contact tracing all over the world with an experienced consultant to manage the customer relations data system, and the Department of Public Health in a joint effort that would offer cities and towns a safety valve if they became overwhelmed. How to do it? We named a dedicated project team at the Massachusetts Health Connector, our health-care insurance exchange, to manage the effort. The collaborative was operational on April 3, 2020, less than two weeks after the decision to launch. Alongside local health efforts, it played a major role in supporting individuals who tested positive as well as their families and other close contacts. Altogether, almost a million people were contacted.

Protect the health-care system

We had watched the devastation in hospitals in Europe, particularly in Italy. People were dying of treatable illnesses because the health-care system was so overwhelmed by Covid patients that it couldn't treat anyone else. I believed that protecting our health-care system from a similar inability to treat strokes, heart attacks, and other emergencies—and to prevent needless suffering and fatalities—was among our highest priorities.

Early on, Marylou and I began having daily calls with hospital CEOs. To protect the health-care system, these calls were thirty-minute round-table discussions with people with knowledge and know-how who could rapidly establish the key facts in order to provide guidance on what to do and how to get it done. The calls included the state's attorney general and covered the topics of the moment: hospital capacity, emergency room activity, staffing concerns, and whatever else the CEOs wanted to raise with us. Those calls turned out to be a particularly valuable line of communication, not just between us and them, but among the CEOs. They offered a powerful example of former competitors collaborating to share vital information on Covid trends, offer spare bed capacity, and collectively discuss what was needed to keep services operating. These were vivid points of pain, which can occur in systems as well as for individuals.

They formed the basis for my decisions early on to support the health-care system by restricting elective procedures, expanding telehealth, establishing field hospitals, and supporting hospitals' abilities to provide surge capacity. We continued to talk regularly and frequently with our hospitals and other health-care partners as we made decisions throughout the pandemic.

Tragedy strikes

As the Commonwealth started the hunt for PPE, launched a testing and tracing infrastructure, and began sorting out our hospital bed capacity, two events changed everything.

The first was the discovery of a developing catastrophe at the Holyoke Soldiers' Home, a state-operated long-term-care facility. Holyoke's mayor, Alex Morse, had received some disturbing reports from staff, and after contacting the facility's superintendent as well as the veterans secretary overseeing the soldiers' home, he elevated his concerns to Lieutenant Governor Polito. Mayor Morse reached out to Karyn on Sunday night, March 29, and she connected him with Secretary Sudders immediately. His observations, which conflicted with earlier reports provided to Secretary Sudders, were deeply alarming. That night, Marylou started to craft an emergency management and staffing plan that would commence the following morning.

The next morning at 7:00, Bennett Walsh, the superintendent of the soldiers' home, was suspended and replaced on an interim basis by Western Mass Hospital CEO Val Liptak, and a contingent of the National Guard arrived to provide nursing and other medical services in the care-management team at that facility for the next several months. The new team did incredible work to blunt the spread of the virus and likely saved many lives. But by then a large number of residents had already been infected. In the end, seventy-six died. Several independent reports were commissioned.

It was the single largest pandemic tragedy at any one location in Massachusetts. I personally called the one hundred families who had lost someone during that spring at Holyoke, whether from Covid or something else, and spoke to about eighty of them. Some of the calls lasted five or ten minutes, but many lasted as long as an hour or more. I learned a great deal about the people who had been taken by Covid, what these families thought of the care at Holyoke, and how losing their loved ones had affected them personally. Many of those conversations were deeply emotional. Although our team acted quickly once we understood the circumstances, we could not undo the tragic consequences.

Overall, we had intensified the efforts related to long-term care facilities and nursing homes. It was no secret that their residents were especially vulnerable. That's why I had already shut down visitation and prioritized the available PPE for long-term-care providers. We began to conduct Covid-surveillance testing in long-term-care facilities.

Almost immediately, the surveillance testing revealed another shocking reality. At a nursing home in Wilmington, a highly respected facility, seventy-seven of ninety-one residents tested positive, even though none of them showed symptoms at that time. The results provided proof that asymptomatic spread was a big problem.

These new facts demanded a major adjustment in our approach. The command center directed $300 million to our long-term-care community and began audits of infection control and safety protocols. But I understood that additional funds and stricter enforcement alone would not be sufficient for facilities that were already stretched and experiencing daily the loss of staff members to Covid. We needed to provide tangible support.

Marylou and I discussed how to proceed, first focusing on the people. She reached out to Lou Wolff, the CEO of Hebrew SeniorLife and a nationally recognized expert, to lead this effort, and to the

Massachusetts Senior Care Association to provide operational support. Their focus was on offering infection-control consultation and training—and staff support—to long-term-care providers across the Commonwealth.

Although case counts and loss of life in our long-term-care community were far too high, the changes we made and the direct support we added decelerated infection and illness in the community over the next several months. We didn't stop measuring results. Infection rates among residents were at zero by the month of July in homes that had previously had high counts.

Helping those who need it the most

Covid-19 was not just ruthless in its attack on people's health, but also held up a harsh mirror to our society, highlighting the fractures and gaps in our government services. From the beginning of my administration. I was always cognizant that core public services needed to work for everyone. For me, the first order of public service is to help those who need it the most—fulfilling government's unique role. That's why we invested immediately in reforming the Department of Children and Families, modernizing the MBTA, fixing a very broken Health Connector, expanding the Earned Income Tax Credit, and reconceiving behavioral health and substance misuse services.

In a matter of weeks as the economy shut down, food insecurity flared. Throughout the months of March, April, and May, we worked side by side with local and federal partners to expand our food acquisition and distribution programs. This came with a series of unique challenges. Food pantries were often staffed by volunteers—often older, retired people who wanted to give back. Many locations were in shared or crowded spaces and involved a lot of close contact. Put those two things together, and suddenly there was a huge shortage of people willing to work on food distribution. And this at exactly the same time schools closed, unemployment skyrocketed, and demand exploded.

I instructed the command center to work with the National Guard, the food banks, and other nonprofit organizations like the Salvation Army to figure out a strategy for delivering food in the short term to those who needed it, which they did and did well. But it would not be enough. In April, Marylou and I asked Steve to work with the command center and our recently established Food Security Task Force to develop a sustainable approach to this issue going forward. Federal financial support was enormously helpful, but we were missing an organized way to address immediate food insecurity needs while expanding operations across the state to meet increasing demand. The task force issued its report on May 17, 2020. It was the first comprehensive review of the system's strengths and weaknesses in years, establishing a strategic approach for investing more than $50 million of state and federal funds into food acquisition and distribution systems, while also expanding access to food stamps and related benefit programs.

This was a solid example of how to use the Results Framework. The food distribution network is fragmented—strong in some places and limited or nonexistent in others. The task force developed a snapshot of how the current system operated and who the key operators were across the state. It then identified major opportunities to improve the system's overall capacity to perform. It asked where state investments in the system—from farms to food banks to fishermen— would make a positive difference long after the pandemic.

A quick word about the role played by the Massachusetts National Guard throughout the pandemic. Simply put, it cannot be overstated. I would turn to these highly trained women and men to tap into their incredibly varied collection of skills to meet our greatest needs—quickly. In what otherwise would have taken weeks if not longer to mobilize, they were prepared. Not only did they have the capabilities to provide medical assistance at Holyoke and had the logistics experience to help feed thousands of families throughout Massachusetts, but these women and men also operated the first large-scale Covid surveillance testing program in long-term care facilities in the country and supported many of our free testing locations across Massachusetts. When the vaccines arrived, the Guard also set up and staffed many of our vaccination sites. In an extremely challenging time, they made an enormous positive difference.

A plan for the economy

To help fight the virus, at first Massachusetts hunkered down. People who could work from home did so, and people who worked in grocery stores, health-care facilities, manufacturing operations, and other businesses deemed essential went to work under unprecedented rules and requirements. Nightlife ceased. Restaurants either pivoted to takeout or delivery or temporarily (sometimes permanently) closed their doors. Streets, trains, buses, airports, houses of worship, funeral homes, gyms, schools, and college campuses sat empty.

The numbers in our Covid hospitalization census had peaked on April 21. In six weeks, fewer than a hundred confirmed cases in Massachusetts and a handful of hospitalizations had grown to thousands of new confirmed cases every day and almost four thousand patients in Massachusetts hospital beds—nearly 40 percent of the state's total inpatient bed capacity.

As case and hospitalization data started to move in the right direction, I began to think about how to reopen. Colleges and schools

Service to Those in Need

Tips Tools and Tactics

Covid-19 magnified the way hardship falls on the most vulnerable and the vital societal role of an effective government. We have found some ways to reach individuals and families in the hardest-hit communities that can be universally applied,

no matter the crisis. These tips are grounded in the power of personal connections.

- **Watch your language.** We are a state and country made up of many nationalities and ethnic groups speaking dozens of languages. Yes, English is still the primary language for most, but it is not the first language of many. Know what languages the residents in your area speak, and be sure to have all materials translated accordingly. Also, make translators available so that people can ask and get answers to their critical questions.

- **Acknowledge the digital opportunity.** Basic services can be made available on a mobile phone or laptop, so that transactions like food stamp applications, health-care alerts, and rental assistance can be readily accessible anywhere, so push these opportunities.

- **Acknowledge the digital divide.** There are two sides of the digital coin. Many individuals and households lack reliable internet access or an understanding of how to use it. Getting to these folks may mean door-to-door outreach or

(continued)

connecting with local community and religious organizations. Here, the power is not an electronic interface; it is the hard work of face-to-face (at safe social distance) contacts and word of mouth.

- **Repeat, repeat, repeat.** The communications gurus will tell you that if you want a shot at anyone hearing your message, you must deliver it at least seven times. And that's just to register an idea. Important messages need real, full-blown, multimedia communications plans (in many languages). Engage expert advice. Allocate time and resources. Seek feedback on what's working and adjust. Use all communications media—digital, phone, paper, billboards, and leaflets.

- **Find trusted speakers.** While it's critical that folks hear from elected leaders, that's just the start of where people get their information. Hold online forums with trusted leaders for specific communities. If necessary, hire help with the outreach to speakers, advertising, and production. (One community enlisted its teens to do the outreach campaign to teens for vaccinations and had outsized success increasing these numbers.)

- **Tap ethnic media.** Many radio, digital, TV, and print media outlets reach audiences in their native languages; many people seek their news from nontraditional sources. These outlets are not expensive and often reach populations that don't tune in to traditional media.

- **Show up—at grocery stores and other places where people gather.** Throughout Covid-19, we set up pop-up testing in neighborhood locations or ad hoc sites to distribute food and supplies (diapers, masks). We also used these alternatives to let people know about contact tracing and vaccinations. Some communities had Covid street fairs. One community set up a vaccination site at a local nightclub on warm summer evenings.

- **Leverage local.** Local community health centers played an instrumental role in all aspects of our Covid-19 response. These employ trusted health professionals who speak multiple languages. Providing funding, PPE, testing materials, and vaccines to these local health centers reaches deep into the community. The same is true for local community groups. Local residents know and rely on these organizations. Providing funding support, information, and supplies offers another way to connect with individuals and families that may be outside the mainstream media and economy. Schools, too, are a natural connection point for information and for vital services.

- **Make it easy, with many sites that are open weekdays, evenings, and weekends.** Be clear that these services are truly open to all and will not impact access to other programs. Free is good. Other incentives may make the difference in attracting new participants.

would remain closed for in-person learning for the rest of the school year; bars, concert halls, and other entertainment venues would not be opening anytime soon. But what about everything else?

Using the Results Framework as a guide and with people are policy as the first step, in late April, I announced a Reopening Advisory Board, to be cochaired by the administration's leads for the economy: Lieutenant Governor Polito and Housing and Economic Development Secretary Michael Kennealy. The board's fifteen members represented various employer communities across Massachusetts and included infectious disease and public health experts, and three mayors. The advisory board was supported by its own dedicated team including staff from Kennealy's office and consultants. I thought that a group of this size would be best suited to engage with the many employment sectors that would want to weigh in on how to safely reopen. This board would coordinate with the command center and medical advisers to translate public health safety standards into business-operation requirements and guidance. Again, urgency drove deadlines. I gave them three weeks to develop a full reopening plan.

On May 18, we released a four-phase plan that would follow public health guidelines—especially regarding PPE, social distancing, cleaning protocols, and capacity limits. Phase one would start with the businesses most likely to succeed in implementing the new rules. If it was deemed successful, phase two would open sectors that needed time to implement and test the new rules. Phase three would make it possible for most of the businesses that were open to do so more completely, with either higher capacity limits or none; it would also bring in some of the businesses that would have the most difficulty operating under rules and guidance. Phase four would cover sectors that needed to remain closed until a vaccine was readily available. Those included bars, nightclubs, concert halls, and large entertainment venues like Boston Garden, home of the Celtics and the Bruins.

Today these phases seem familiar, but a lot of heavy lifting was required to imagine this for the first time. By the time Covid hospitalizations and case counts had begun to decline, in late April, more than three thousand Massachusetts residents had died from the virus. But just sixty days after I issued the original emergency order, the beginnings of a full-blown Covid-surveillance infrastructure were in place, and we had reopening guidance, supported by our medical advisers, that most employers could work with. Our hospitals were in a much better place than they'd been in just weeks earlier, and our work with congregate and long-term-care communities had boosted their capacity to keep staffers and residents safe.

The Struggle to Reopen
(June 2020–December 2020)

As some businesses began to reopen, we held our collective breath. The early stages were encouraging. Massachusetts case counts, hospitalizations, and deaths continued to decline throughout the summer. People accepted the idea that they needed to wear masks if they were working or shopping indoors. And although not everyone was pleased with the phased approach, the reopening plan continued its step-by-step implementation.

I began to think about the fall. No one knew what the next ten days, much less the next ten weeks, would bring. But in June and July, states in the South began experiencing increases in cases, hospitalizations, and fatalities. Clearly, Covid would not just go away. With a potential second surge in the wings, I asked Marylou and Kristen what we needed to add to our arsenal of what to do and the best way to execute how to do it. That led us to focus on three key initiatives:

- Expand and improve access to testing.

- Develop plans for K–12 and higher education reopening.

- Prepare for expiration of the moratorium on housing evictions.

A massive increase in testing

One precept of the Results Framework is to expect Murphy's law. Part of pushing for results is constant evaluation and adjustment. Even with the decreasing number of cases over the early summer, I knew that we needed to learn more about Covid and its reach. Testing would provide that critical data. The Commonwealth's testing capacity had continued to expand, from eight thousand tests a day in April to twelve thousand a day in May. Throughout the summer, the daily rate increased, but the trajectory was not fast enough. Marylou and I believed we needed to achieve fifty to seventy thousand tests a day. To get there, we would have to do something different. In discussions with our Medical Advisory Board, Eric Lander offered to dramatically expand the Broad Institute's low-cost, high-speed Covid test-processing capacity—if the state could help pay for the additional equipment needed. I readily agreed. This highly respected nonprofit was our best option. Along with a full set of public health precautions, including masks, physical distancing, and capacity limits, testing and tracing were the linchpin in our battle against Covid.

Within a matter of weeks, the Broad had set up a new Covid test center for two main purposes. Its first purpose would be to support the growth of our Stop the Spread campaign to provide free tests in many of the communities that were most affected by Covid.

Second, with the added volume, we had gained test-processing for the hundred-plus colleges and universities in the state. The board's partnership with colleges in the Commonwealth was unlike anything anywhere else in the country. Combined with the testing protocols that our higher education institutions had put in place, this capacity created affordable, regular, and robust testing for college students, staff members, and faculties throughout the fall semester. A few schools did their own contact tracing, but most relied on their local health boards and the Community Tracing Collaborative to do the work for them. We had some high-stakes moments as college students returned, but the worst-case scenario that some had predicted did not materialize.

By September, we were processing more than fifty thousand tests a day. By November, that number had grown to eighty thousand. The push not only made Massachusetts one of the very top testers with fast turnaround in the country, but also gave us the facts we needed to understand Covid's trajectory and what to do about it.

Reopening the schools

Preparing to reopen K–12 schools was both profoundly important and profoundly complex. We were talking about our children and their education and welfare, and we were navigating layers of decision-making among local school boards, superintendents, the teachers unions, and ultimately, parents. Even with significant new state and federal funding, the variation across public school districts about the right way to approach the fall term was tremendous.

In May, with schools closed for the remainder of the year, I reached out to Jeff Riley, commissioner of the Department of Elementary and Secondary Education, to talk about plans for the upcoming school year. Once again, I was concentrating on people as the first step. Jeff was a former teacher, a former superintendent of a large urban school district, and a fighter for public education. His senior leadership team had already pivoted to focus 100 percent on what it would take to open schools safely but would need additional help.

For medical expertise, Jeff engaged an infectious disease specialist at Massachusetts General Hospital and a pediatrician who was leading the Massachusetts chapter of the US Academy of Pediatrics. And to support his team with the drafting of polices and guidance, preparing communications, and project management, staff from other agencies and consultants were added to the team. Steve, too, provided direct support to Jeff and his team.

The fact-gathering got underway immediately, detailing the points of pain that schools were facing, especially in lower-income urban areas where space was insufficient to meet distancing guidelines, older buildings lacked adequate ventilation, and always-confounding bus transportation met new challenges in a Covid world. The medical experts and consultants were getting out of the tower, gathering the latest on what other states and countries were doing through in-depth reviews of the medical literature and scientific journals.

By the middle of July, Jeff's team had developed guidelines and advisories for safely opening the schools. They considered three scenarios: a full return to in-person learning; a hybrid of in-person and remote learning; fully remote learning, with no in-person classroom experience. Each school system was required to develop plans for each option to prepare for changing Covid dynamics in its community.

While other states provided similar high-level guidance, our intense follow-the-facts approach provided the platform for very detailed advisories and protocols. We looked at the best medical science, incorporated what was working in other places around the country and world, and paid attention to the specific circumstances in our most challenging communities. For example, the Department of Elementary and Secondary Education did a review of the data on whether or not there was a difference in Covid transmission between six feet of distance or three. After sharing it with the Medical Advisory Board, which signed off on the research, the department issued guidelines indicating that while six feet physical distancing between students and staff was preferred, three feet was acceptable, according to World Health Organization standards. Months later, the CDC made a similar recommendation. The three-feet advice was a game changer, especially for older, urban facilities and for bus transportation. Throughout the summer, the department provided an extraordinary amount of guidance and technical assistance to support the implementation, including for sports and other extracurricular activities, labs, and music.

This work described what to do. The next piece, how to do it, was the domain of the local districts. Typically, each one determined how its schools would operate—and defended that role fiercely. Yes, districts had to follow state requirements for things such as number of days and hours taught and statewide competency exams. But local school boards and superintendents decided the operational details, and their budgets were set by other local officials. While every bone in my body wanted to impose as much in-person learning as was safely possible, at this time, in discussions with Commissioner Riley, I felt that local officials needed to make their own decisions about which scenario made the most sense for their staff and students. Local leaders would determine the details of how our students would attend school in the fall.

By September, about 40 percent of the public school districts had returned to school on a remote basis, with 60 percent relying on a hybrid system with limited in-person learning. But almost all private and parochial schools were in-person from the start of the 2020–2021 school year, and they were experiencing very little Covid, even when operating in communities with significant Covid case counts. Most of them used the same guidance for in-person learning that had been issued by the department. Unfortunately, their positive experience didn't result in a more significant return to in-person learning in the public schools.

But we didn't give up trying. Twice a week, my core Covid leadership team, including Marylou, Kristen, Tim, Karen, and me, would meet with Jeff and his team to review emerging data and opportunities to get as many of our kids back to in-person learning as quickly as possible. We were continually evaluating what tools we had available and how to implement them most effectively, including funding and access to PPE and ventilation equipment. In addition, Commissioner Riley's team set up a Covid help hotline dedicated to support school administrators. Later in the year, Jeff's office made available an innovative, first-in-the-nation pooled testing program for schools, which was free and open to all school districts. And when vaccines became available, more than a hundred free clinics were set up in schools across the state.

With each action, we made some progress. We are all indebted to the superintendents and school leaders who made it work, and I hope that we have all gained an understanding of what it will take to do better for our kids going forward. However, that so many of our students lost so much of the school year was a major disappointment.

Stemming collateral damage: homelessness

In 2020, as summer turned to fall, my office began planning for the expiration of the moratorium on housing evictions that had been in place at the state level since the beginning of the pandemic in March.

We joined a series of meetings with the courts, local officials, affordable housing operators, advocates, and landlords' organizations. Some stated bluntly that lifting the moratorium would create a tsunami of despair, misery, and catastrophe. Our team's fact review was mixed on the magnitude of the impact. While some reports inferred sweeping disruption, other information predicted far less impact. In all scenarios, however, it was clear that the loss of jobs during the pandemic threatened an increase in homelessness, and the subsequent potential for further Covid transmission. Here was another example of not only the destructive impact of Covid-19 beyond direct health, but also the role of government services to the vulnerable. Housing has been at the top of my administration's agenda, including expanding housing opportunities and addressing homelessness. Any sustainable plan for reopening had to include housing and homelessness prevention as priorities.

The next step would be to put together a team. My chief legal counsel, Bob Ross, and the housing and economic development undersecretary, Jennifer Maddox, would lead the team. Bob's relationship with the courts was crucial to the success of the effort because they conducted the eviction hearings. Jennifer and her office were responsible for all things related to housing in our administration. The rest of the dedicated team tapped existing talent at the Department of Housing and Community Development and supplemented that with staffers from the governor's office, other agencies, and consultants. I also asked Steve to work closely with Bob, Jennifer, and the team to help develop the organizational structure and accelerate the key decisions needed.

With the team established, the first part of following the facts was to determine the size of the problem: How many people should we be worried about, given trends around eviction hearings, emergency housing, and rental assistance? The second part of the fact set was to scrutinize how our community partners used available programs to help people who were eligible to remain in their homes. The third part involved speaking to housing advocates, local community groups, and landlords to understand their personal stories, their points of pain. In just a few weeks, we developed a package of initiatives of what to do to address the oncoming problem.

In October, I announced a $170 million state Eviction Diversion Initiative—made possible by an unprecedented increase in rental assistance from the state legislature, and a major expansion of state-supported legal services. Two things immediately became clear. First, our program was unprepared for the increase in applications, and second, the rules, and especially the performance metrics around managing the workload, needed a major upgrade. The team had developed a straightforward approach to what to do, but now we had to get creative about how. Quickly, the team streamlined the application process, provided direct support to our community partners, expanded outreach efforts, and developed a comprehensive performance dashboard to assess daily progress.

By December, the backlog of rental-assistance applications was still growing. The current interventions were not enough. I decided to move forward with a state-funded, privately operated, virtual rental-assistance application center. It would provide additional processing capacity for our community partners, just as the Community Tracing Collaborative supported local boards of health with contact tracing. It reduced application backlogs and could adjust its workload based on which community partners were having the toughest time keeping up.

In January, the federal government established a significant rental-assistance program, allocating more than $400 million to Massachusetts. We stumbled for a short while as we adjusted to the new rules and anticipated expansion of the program and made some adjustments in the project's governance, but by March—through a neat data match with other state agencies to simplify eligibility, along with further streamlining and new processing capacity—we were approving as many applications in one month as had been approved during the entire year pre-Covid. The eviction diversion effort, from October to March, made for a 150-day demonstration of a key precept of the Results Framework: measure, evaluate, adjust, and repeat. We kept looking at the performance results, talking to those on the ground, and made subsequent policy and operational improvements to mitigate a major problem and provide thousands of individuals and families with a safe, predictable place to live.

As we write, in the late fall of 2021, the Eviction Diversion Initiative continues to keep people in their homes. Fewer people are seeking assistance from our emergency services, transitional housing, and shelter programs than at any point in recent history, and the court activity related to evictions is as low as it has been in years. Moreover, as federal funds began to flow to states, many were not positioned to put those dollars to work. However, Massachusetts was a top-ten performer. For me, this a textbook example of why it's so critical not just to focus on what to do (provide funds), but to continually improve how to do it by measuring results and making necessary adjustments—quickly.

Further, as we were addressing this housing issue, we realized that many very small businesses in these same hard-hit communities were teetering on the edge. Most of these were owner-operated shops, often neighborhood retailers or restaurants, and by the end of 2020, many were not sure they would make it. While the federal Paycheck Protection Program succeeded to keep many employers viable and their employees paid, a fact review showed that there were many Massachusetts small businesses that for a variety of reasons saw no benefit. Not only were these the small businesses that make up the rhythm of our neighborhood main streets, they provided paychecks to help with daily living, including food and rent.

To address this problem, we worked with the legislature to create a very small business assistance program. At the beginning of 2021, the program launched with a focus on very small, women-, minority-, and veteran-owned businesses. In about 100 days, this targeted program provided $700 million in grants to over 15,000 small businesses. It was the largest initiative of its kind in the country. Overall, almost half the businesses that received these grants were owned by women, 43 percent were owned by people of color, and the majority operated in communities hardest hit by the pandemic.

Progress isn't linear

One thing Covid-19 has made abundantly clear is that the worst crises are not short-term events; they persist. But that doesn't mean we stop applying the framework. As 2020 came to an end, with colder weather and more people huddling indoors, the case count continued to climb. Thankfully, the curve was flatter and more drawn out than what we had seen in the spring.

Thanksgiving was both predictable and unfortunate. Despite all our messaging, I knew it would be very hard for people to stay apart, given the isolation and anxiety of the previous eight months. Indeed, seven days after Thanksgiving, Covid case counts and hospitalizations started to climb significantly. They continued to rise throughout the holiday season, peaking in mid-January, on the heels of Christmas and New Year's.

The Thanksgiving spike forced us to adjust. We temporarily suspended some high-risk activities, put additional constraints on restaurants and other formal gathering sites, and required early closing hours for many businesses. It all made for a very somber week between Christmas and New Year's Day.

On New Year's Eve, my wife and I spent some time in a neighbor's open garage with two couples who had been part of our bubble throughout the pandemic. We had not spent any time inside with one another but had sat in our backyards around a firepit (how many of those were sold during Covid?), walked together in the woods and along the trails in state parks, and dined outdoors on several occasions. Around midnight, my wife and I took a long walk home. We walked along the ocean's edge on a boardwalk that runs parallel to one of the major arteries in and out of Swampscott and Marblehead. We did not see a single person or a single car. The tide was all the way out. It was completely silent, and it was bizarre.

The Race to Vaccinate (December 2020—Fall 2021)

Since spring 2020, the governors had been having weekly calls with Vice President Pence and other members of the Trump administration's Covid-19 Task Force. Testing, equipment, CDC guidance, and case counts were the typical topics. As cases and hospitalizations climbed across the country during the fall, our conversations eventually turned to Operation Warp Speed, the federal government's $10 billion investment in accelerating vaccine development.

In October, the feds told us that they expected to meet their end-of-the-year deadline for delivering a vaccine, and a few weeks later, Pfizer issued public statements about the early results of its clinical trials. Details of timing, supply, production, distribution, and the like still had to be worked out. But it was becoming evident that a vaccine could be available by the end of the year.

Invoking people are policy, our leadership team formed a Vaccine Advisory Group to help our administration prepare to distribute the vaccine once it became available. The group was composed of medical professionals, public health experts, elected officials, and community leaders. I wanted to know what the best way would be to save lives. I wanted the group to focus particularly on how to equitably allocate, distribute, and administer the shots.

Around that same time, I announced a high-level phased plan to administer vaccines for all state residents. Although we were still light on many details from DC, including the impact of the transition in the White House, it was essential to give the public some idea of what to expect. Following the counsel of the Vaccine Advisory Group, phase one would run from December to February and would cover health-care personnel, home health workers, first responders, and congregate-care residents and staff. Phase two, from February to April, would begin with residents over the age of 75, and include essential workers, residents over 65, and people with ongoing medical conditions. After the initial announcement, I moved educators up on the priority list to help get our kids in school. Phase three, from April forward, would include "everyone else" adults 18 years and older.

As phase one began, we used multiple paths to administer the vaccines, in big central locations and in smaller facilities across the state. Hospitals received the lion's share of doses, because they had the most people to vaccinate and were equipped to handle the deep-freeze storage requirements. We used a host of mobile providers to assist us with the residents and staffers in congregate care, which includes homeless shelters and residential facilities for those dealing with addiction, behavioral health, and developmental disability issues. We provided community health centers with vaccines and the first of several rounds of funding to support their efforts. And we chose to vaccinate correctional inmates and staffers, because prisons meet the definition of a congregate-care setting. Some people thought this was controversial. I did not.

Time to reevaluate and reset

We had a policy approach and a plan to implement, but instead of being welcomed by the public, it fell flat. Performance was not matching public expectations. For many people in Massachusetts, the eligibility rules were frustrating and infuriating. Worry about their own vulnerability to Covid was amplified by the arrival—*finally*—of an answer to their concerns. They felt they deserved to be vaccinated quickly and didn't want to get sick when proven protection was so close at hand. Friends of mine who were neither old nor physically frail began to call me up and explain why they belonged in phase one. They had friends in Florida who had been able to "cut through the red tape" and get vaccinated there, and they couldn't understand why they couldn't do the same thing here. No explanation about fairness, science, vulnerability, or process changed their view. Mayors, local elected officials, and state legislators began getting similar calls from their constituents. Every decision we had made about the rollout was being challenged. Even though the phase-one launch was just underway, we needed to listen to the very real points of pain and adjust.

Then, in late January, unhappiness about the timeline exploded when it became clear that Massachusetts was not administering its vaccines as quickly as other states were. There were reasonable explanations about our performance to date. But the performance of other states made our team reevaluate our approach. In my conversations with other governors, I asked what they had put in place to get such strong results, and I asked Marylou and her team to reach out to their peers in other states. It was clear that if we were going to move as quickly as we needed to, the initial plans to make this a purely local administration process wouldn't work. It was time to reevaluate and reset the approach.

The model we landed on employed a mix of methods. The team determined that instead of the locally administered vaccinations in each Massachusetts community that earlier plans had outlined, sites that met certain volume, operating, and reporting standards would serve more people quickly. Speed mattered. The vaccine plan shifted, and the command center organized mass vaccination sites around the Commonwealth—at places like Fenway Park and Gillette Stadium, as well as other locations across the state, including the Natick Mall and the former Circuit City in Dartmouth—that could serve thousands of people a day. In addition, hospitals and health-care providers that met volume requirements would be permitted to vaccinate their patients as well as their employees. We provided community health centers with additional resources, including support from the National Guard, to administer vaccines to their patients and the people who lived in their communities. At the same time, the federal government dramatically expanded its retail pharmacy network program, adding hundreds of privately operated sites across the Commonwealth. Altogether, those adjustments meant that we went big and fast but also small and regional.

In the end, the revised model worked well. Larger sites, regional collaboratives, retail pharmacies, and provider groups moved far more vaccines, faster, than a complicated, purely local solution would have. By the beginning of March, we were in the top ten among all states in the percent of our population that had been vaccinated. By the middle of April, we were either first or second among all states in the percent of our population that had been vaccinated—a status we traded back and forth with Vermont for most of the rest of the year.

But in our desire to quickly meet the growing anxiety of residents about access to the vaccines, we made those adjustments without vetting them carefully with other elected officials. Most had anticipated that the vaccines would be administered through local boards of health, as had been done historically. For many local officials and state legislators, our change in approach wasn't just a communications flub—it was a sudden and significant departure from expectations. And no one, especially not an elected official in a time like this and on an issue like this, wanted to be surprised. In balancing speed and process, I knew this was a time when faster was imperative to respond to the public demand and save lives. But I clearly underestimated the importance of the change to other elected officials—and they didn't hesitate to let me know.

On top of the surging pent-up demand, the feds' forecast of vaccine supply was far too optimistic. I was working on the assumption that, as the federal government had indicated, we would have all the vaccines we needed by February. That did not happen. Supply didn't catch up with demand until late April. Each state's allocation was only a week's worth at a time and—even worse—just a nominal amount compared with the overall need. In short, we could make available only a fraction of the needed doses each week to the millions who had been waiting for months.

In addition, while a few other states had developed a vaccine pre-registration system, Massachusetts had not. I just missed this. Our vaccine appointment website worked reasonably well during phase one, but in February, when the website opened for phase two, it crashed immediately, unable to handle the huge volume. Sixty thousand people managed that day to schedule vaccination appointments for the following week, but for many others, frustrating hours spent fruitlessly chasing an appointment on a confounding website was a breaking point. I had failed to follow my own advice on launching a website, and the crowd roared its disapproval!

When you fail . . .

After one well-publicized fix to the system proved to be no better in making it easier to line up a vaccine appointment, leaving thousands deeply disappointed after many hours of effort, Marylou and the command center expanded the partnership with our Executive Office of Technology Services and Security. Its first task was to address capacity on the existing website to ensure that it would work regardless of volume. Technology Services simultaneously took the lead on building a preregistration system. As with other initiatives, we needed people with experience and know-how. Technology Services rapidly created a team of outside vendors and internal advisers to strengthen the website and dive into building the preregistration site.

I stayed very close to those efforts, talking with the teams every day. While this work was going on, and despite the creaky website, people were getting appointments and our vaccine delivery model continued to perform.

However, it was still just too difficult for too many people to get an appointment and get vaccinated. We needed a simple online preregistration system—one that worked. On March 12, 2021, we launched the site. I followed the traffic on social media for the first hour or so and then relaxed. Tech Services had succeeded. The website was working exactly as intended. From that point forward, it was all fairly anti-climactic. People who couldn't access a vaccine through some other channel went to the preregistration site, got their appointments scheduled within two weeks, and got vaccinated.

By the end of April, the supply from the feds had finally caught up with demand, and the challenge became reaching those who were unvaccinated for whatever reason. It was an all-out push in multiple languages and mediums. We knocked on doors, partnered with churches and other faith-based groups, continued to support community health centers, and collaborated with other leading local organizations. By the middle of May, it was pretty clear that we would hit our goal of 4.1 million people fully vaccinated by mid-June.

On June 22, 2021, we reached the target I had set the previous December to vaccinate 75 percent of Massachusetts residents over eighteen years old. It was a moment to pause and reflect. I knew there was much more to do, but we had climbed that hill. I tweeted out the news. Shortly afterward, the *Boston Globe* blared, "Massachusetts Hits Milestone of 4.1 Million People Fully Vaccinated; US to Miss Mark." Little did we understand the portent of that headline in terms of who was vaccinated. In the months ahead, we would understand all too well.

After a bumpy start, Massachusetts was a leader among states in vaccination administration. Back in December, as the vaccination campaign began, reaching that goal had seemed aspirational. Thousands of new Covid cases were being discovered every day, more than two thousand Covid patients were in our hospitals, hundreds of thousands of people were still out of work, many schools remained closed for in-person learning, and fatalities continued to climb at an alarming rate. Questions of vaccine production, supply, and distribution were everywhere. On the day we hit that vaccination target, Massachusetts had only thirty-three new Covid cases, just over a hundred Covid patients hospitalized, and one new death.

Alpha, Beta, Gamma, Delta

In June, we all breathed a sigh of relief—but only one. Until we had met vaccination targets across the nation—and the world—I had said that Covid was a lot like Michael Myers from the *Halloween* movies. It just never dies.

By July, the Delta variant had arrived in the United States. Globally, in places with limited vaccination rates, this Covid variant was a terror. But in Great Britain, which had a high vaccination rate, although cases climbed, hospitalizations and deaths did not, even as the government reopened the country. The same phenomenon began to play out across the United States. Although the Delta variant was driving increases in case counts nationwide, hospitalizations and deaths were rising dramatically only in states with lower vaccination rates and marginally in states with higher vaccination rates. There were some breakthrough Delta cases in vaccinated people, but the vaccines worked. With limited exceptions, most fully vaccinated people did not get seriously sick, and their chances of being hospitalized or dying of Covid remained exceedingly low.

In Massachusetts, we continued the outreach to unvaccinated residents. Our efforts in the hardest-hit communities were paying off. Lower-income, densely populated cities like Chelsea were outperforming the state average in terms of vaccinating its citizens. By August 2021, more than 60 percent of Black residents and 56 percent of Hispanics were vaccinated compared to 35 percent and 41 percent nationally. There was more to do, but we had made meaningful progress.

As summer ended, we continued to monitor the medical science, and the overwhelming evidence showed vaccines were proving their efficacy. I mandated vaccinations for all residents and staffers in our long-term-care facilities and for the more than forty thousand employees and contractors in the state's executive branch. I was thrilled when the FDA gave its final approval to the Pfizer vaccine for those sixteen and older. I had read reports and heard from some people directly that they wanted to get past the emergency-use-authorization stage before they got vaccinated.

Later, as soon as the federal approvals were in place, we jumped right in to make vaccines readily available to our younger teens and children five years and older, and the same with vaccine boosters. By the end of November, 86 percent of all Massachusetts residents had at least one dose and 71 percent were fully vaccinated.[1]

. . .

As we write in the late fall of 2021, Covid will be a dominant feature in the public policy landscape for the foreseeable future—in our nation and across the world. There will be other variants, and debate over the best way to handle them will continue. However, it is crystal clear that vaccines are our most effective weapon against the virus. The goal must be to get as many people as possible vaccinated—to protect the more vulnerable among us from getting Covid in the first place, and to make it possible for our schools to stay open, our businesses to operate, and our health-care system to function so that our lives can move on—everywhere.

We tell this story because the Results Framework guided us in many elements of my administration's response to Covid. The work we did on testing, tracing, long-term care, eviction avoidance, and vaccination all built on the framework's key elements. We always start with people, and the leadership and governance model of the Covid-19 Response Command Center, a high powered dedicated team, was foundational for our ability to perform. For all this work, I insisted on understanding the facts, the points of pain, and what others were doing, not only for my leadership team, but for everyone involved. All our efforts were then focused on what and how: delivering solutions by maximizing existing programs and facilities as well as creating new ones. Everyone working on the state's Covid response understood the importance of measuring results. We pored over analytics and metrics dashboards for insight and decision-making.

Operations rarely go exactly as we hope they will. Crises are by their nature complex, unpredictable, and frustrating. It's critical to have a tested method, to communicate honestly, to pivot quickly when facts on the ground change, to measure how you are doing, to have the humility to make adjustments and keep going.

The tragedy of Covid is profound. The facts are horrific. As we write now in fall 2021, more than 5.1 million people worldwide have died, including 770,000 in the United States and more than 19,000 in Massachusetts. A generation of schoolchildren lost much of a year of learning and support for their emotional growth. The sickness, job loss, and family disruption will have an impact for years to come.

I can only hope this experience prepares us for what lies ahead. As Nelson Mandela said, "After climbing a great hill, one only finds there are many more to climb."

EPILOGUE

Possibility

I n January 2015, faith leaders at Congregación León de Judá, Boston's largest Spanish-speaking Protestant church, hosted me for the most memorable event of my inauguration. One by one, a dozen or so ministers, rabbis, priests, and other religious leaders spoke to more than a thousand attendees who filled the massive modern sanctuary in Roxbury.

"We will be partnering with you, we will be praying with you, we want you to use us as a resource, as allies, as people who would want to be there in moments of need, to provide whatever counsel we can provide from our spiritual perspective," said Rev. Roberto Miranda, the leader of the Protestant church.[1]

Others offered eloquent blessings for our new administration. Each brief speech registered like another wave of forward-looking support.

When it was my turn to respond, I reflected on my desire to serve the public, offering the passage from Philippians 2:3 that is my lodestar: "Do nothing out of selfish ambition or vain conceit. Rather, in humility value others above yourselves."

At the end of the event, the faith leaders asked me and my wife, Lauren, along with Karyn Polito and her husband, Steve, to come to the front of the room. There, they huddled around us, wrapping us in the center of a tight circle of long robes, black suits, yarmulkes, and prayer caps. Then they offered private, quiet words of encouragement. That moment of different perspectives and common hopes launched our administration.

It was astonishingly beautiful: all that positive energy wrapped *literally* and figuratively in a cloak of faith and fellowship. I've never forgotten it. When stuff gets real, and the path forward seems lonely and unfair, I summon the optimism of that moment. People were with us. They believed in us. And they expected us to do our very best. They never said we wouldn't falter or make mistakes—only that they would be there to help us get back up if we did. And they have been there—over and over again. Our pledge to serve has been tied to their commitment to share the load. For that I am forever grateful.

Dwell in Possibility

Over the course of my almost twenty years of service in state and local government, I've evolved what you might call a philosophy of public service. It is expressed when I'm called to give colleagues a pep talk. I start by defining the challenge: solve problems for people, all the time. Some solutions involve short-term, transactional problems, and some involve directional change that takes a long time and lasts for years or sometimes decades.

This work is complicated, and the stakes are high. The way government operates, by design, is bound by laws and protocols, making it quirky, hard to change, and not always built for the speed of the twenty-first century. Any shift makes for a battle against the status quo that can pull even the best ideas down to earth. The decisions involve potential winners and losers—in a very public sphere—who are ready to engage in a fight. And because this is the *public* sector, all of it is done openly amid a clamor of journalists, bloggers, commentators, and social media mavens.

That is why no one in public service should expect to come through the experience without a few cuts and bruises. To many of our observers in the public and in the media, we will never be any better than the worst 5 percent of our colleagues on their worst days. The circumstances surrounding the incidents they call out may be small and easily dealt with or they might reveal systemic failures that need to be addressed. And because we are human, they might be a result of the disappointments of human character. It is up to us to know the difference and to look at our own flaws and fumbles.

But it's also up to us to understand that many of those incidents don't deserve the airtime or the ink they receive. It's incumbent on us to push back against spurious narratives about government's failure to work. Because government *can* and *does* work. Our attention is best put on how we are doing and where we are going, measured against where we were and how we were doing six months or a year ago. Organizational performance gets better, or it gets worse. Our job is to accurately grasp where we are, how to keep improving, and what to communicate about both to people in the communities we serve.

We are in the problem-solving business, and that business is iterative. Times change, tools change, context changes, expectations change, impact changes. As my father always said, "Success is never final." It moves as we move. The better we get, the higher the bar goes. The failures we experience must be learning opportunities. As long as we stay humble about the constantly changing context in which we operate, as long as we stay focused on our commitment to get better, and as long as we keep in touch with the people we work with and serve, the public will be with us. The noise of the day-to-day is usually driven by a fundamental reality: it's easy, and indeed expected, to howl about the worst failures of our worst colleagues. Don't listen to *that*. Stay focused on the problems to be solved. We should "dwell in possibility," a phrase from the Massachusetts poet Emily Dickinson, who could imagine a house defined not so much by its elaborate chambers and windows and doors as by the wide-open sky.

Success is about possibility. It blooms when we seize the chance to make something work and envision something more—to get beyond the headlines and the media noise and into that place where we can make something better than it was before. If you set the tone, communicate the task, and speak to the results, taxpayers, customers, and regular people who touch or are touched by their government will see that it can work for them. They will become investors in our collective success.

Protect Our Democracy

Our purpose in presenting the Results Framework is simple: to improve government performance in the delivery of public services. Performance is about results, not in the abstract but in how individuals, families, businesses, and other entities experience those results. Good government services are not just what we should expect; they are necessary to nurture and protect our democracy. Faulty services are not just frustrating; they are undermining. When we deliver results and report them honestly to constituents, we build trust in government and public institutions. When we fail, we hurt ourselves and the people we seek to serve, and we undermine their belief in the institutions we represent.

Amy Lerman, a political scientist at the University of California, Berkeley, expresses this in her book *Good Enough for Government Work*:

The wisdom from much of the political science research is that partisanship trumps everything, but one of the insights from the policy feedback literature in particular is that when people experience policy, they don't necessarily experience it as partisans. They experience it as a parent sending their child to school or a patient visiting a doctor, not as a Democrat or Republican. And because people are often thinking in nonpolitical terms during their day-to-day lives, they are much more open to having their views changed when they see the actual, tangible benefits of a policy in their lives. It's a way of breaking through partisanship. . . . The best thing we can do right now to reduce levels of anger and frustration on both sides of the aisle is to give people the things they need to live better lives.[2]

Democracy is imperfect, and it's messy. It involves the kind of intense engagement among people that most of us would never want to see at our own kitchen table, much less day after day in the media. Combine that with the inescapable twenty-four-hour news cycle that needs clicks to survive, the partisan organizations and social media platforms that use anger and outrage to feed their own growth, and the never-ending stories about how government overpromises and underperforms. You end up with a toxic brew that breeds factionalism, cynicism, and mistrust.

In their book *Presidents, Populism, and the Crisis of Democracy*, the political scientists William Howell and Terry Moe write, "Populists don't just feed on socioeconomic discontent. They feed on ineffective government—and their great appeal is that they claim to replace it with a government that is effective through their own autocratic power."[3]

The *how* of government is usually a lot less fun than the *why* or the *what*. It involves real budgets, real operating assumptions, real metrics, real people, and all the real complexity associated with try-ing to turn someone's big or small idea into practical, sustainable reality. But in the end, it is also what sustains the public's trust and prevents the kind of meltdown we've seen play out again and again, in places large and small throughout this country, over the past several years. The Covid-19 pandemic raised everyone's anxiety level, but it also forced us to see more clearly that by not focusing on the how of governing, we are undermining our larger vision for government generally, along with people's trust in our ability to perform.

Build Trust

When managed with intelligence and compassion—and, yes, a reli-able method—government can be a solution to many of our prob-lems. In fact, it is the *only* solution to some of our problems. Caring for vulnerable children, providing health insurance to the poor, cre-ating reliable transit options for workers, even establishing broad-band service that doesn't produce a return on capital but enables growth for all—these are incredibly hard things to do. Yet they are part of the essential job of government. In 2020 and 2021, the expe-rience of trying to keep citizens safe during a global pandemic drove home how much our lives and our livelihoods depend on local, state, and national governments that work—and that work for us.

But government must succeed at these vexing tasks (and even at less-vexing ones) not just because that is its responsibility. It must do so in an efficient and compassionate way because public trust depends on it. Effective public services are part of the implicit con-tract between the people and its government, and there are many examples about how well it can and does work.

Special Salute to Those
Who Answered the Call

Over the years, I've had the extraordinary privilege of working with many outstanding people in both the private and the public sectors. The best are not only very good at what they do, but have a sense of purpose that is beyond themselves. It's a quiet selflessness that emanates from the belief in the human community, the commonwealth. From the private organization providing care to the public servant, their work is a manifestation of public service. During Covid, I witnessed daily this personal sacrifice in the most harrowing of circumstances for the common good—and it reinforced my belief that the best of public service is the best of America.

The Massachusetts National Guard

Throughout the course of this pandemic, the Massachusetts National Guard has come every time it's been called. And it has exceeded all expectations. The Guard provided critical care services at the Holyoke Soldiers' Home, conducted the first Covid surveillance-testing program at long-term-care facilities in the country, supported community health centers with Covid testing and vaccination programs, and even drove school buses. The Guard also supported local communities, law enforcement, and peaceful demonstrators throughout the difficult summer of 2020 following the horrific murder of George Floyd, provided critical assistance in extinguishing drought-driven forest fires in western Massachusetts, and collected and distributed hundreds of thousands of pieces of PPE to frontline workers. And in the midst of Covid, they protected the Capitol in the aftermath of the attack on January 6, 2021.

In the spring of 2021, when I was in Washington, DC, for meetings with federal officials, I visited the Massachusetts National Guard crew that had been deployed to the nation's capital for several months. About 450 citizen soldiers were there. They met me on the steps of the Capitol—ten to fifteen rows of men and women in uniform standing at attention. I chatted with a few of the ones down front and then posed with the group for a picture. I was so moved by their presence, given all they had done in the previous year, that I said I would stand by the steps and shake hands with anyone who wanted to say hello, just so I could say thank-you.

A few passed on the opportunity, but the vast majority chose to accept. I asked them where they were from, how long they'd been with the Guard, and why they had joined. I took pictures with about half of them. The process lasted a lot longer than I had thought it would—more than ninety minutes—but it was worth every second. Here they were, right in front of me, men and women in their late teens to their late fifties, from all over the Commonwealth, representing multiple races, religions, and ethnicities, with a host of reasons for joining the Guard, all wearing the same uniform and committed to the same mission. *E Pluribus Unum*—out of many, one. It brought tears to my eyes.

Care teams

At any given time, tens of thousands of adults and children in Massachusetts are homeless, or have addiction and behavioral health issues, or suffer developmental disabilities, or simply find themselves at the end of their rope. For them, Covid-19 has been a very real existential threat. Caregivers in the public and private sectors have worked collaboratively throughout the pandemic to do their utmost to keep those people safe.

I recently ran into one of the long-standing leaders of the community of mental health service providers—a guy who is never afraid to tell me when we are underperforming. He pulled me aside and said, "I cannot believe the job your team did throughout this pandemic to support the people on our team and the people we serve. I kept thinking there is no political gain for you to focus so intensely on the people we serve, and yet there you were—every day and in every way. It was amazing."

While I appreciated his praise, and certainly let it sink in, my greatest pleasure was in knowing that it was directed not at me but at the many teams of real people who never gave up, who kept helping people who needed their help. And that was by no means the only praise I heard. Similar comments have come from many people who work in this community. Sometimes the best that we do gets no attention at all. But sometimes it does get the notice it deserves from the people it matters to the most.

Health-care workers, first responders, transit workers, correctional officers

When the pandemic began, there was a lot of talk about "essential businesses." The term came out of the federal government's desire to separate private organizations that had to remain open from those that did not. Health-care providers, grocery stores, pharmacies, manufacturing operations, and the like all needed to be accessible.

For health-care workers, the effects of the pandemic had never let up. When the Covid numbers dropped, patients who had put off their necessary care came back to the hospitals and doctors' offices in large numbers. Though I have spent a big part of my professional career in and around health care, I have been amazed by the grace, discipline, and commitment to the calling we have witnessed from our health-care workers over the past twenty months. It's private-sector work, but it has been profoundly public service. In the public sector, "essential" meant that correctional officers still had to go to work. Police officers, emergency-management personnel, and firefighters had to stay on the job. Forest rangers, public park operators, health-care workers, and a host of other public-sector employees could not work remotely. From the first day of Covid, before we'd acquired adequate knowledge, testing infrastructure, or gear, they had to cover their shifts, twenty-four hours a day, seven days a week. They continued to cruise their assigned routes, work at their job sites, support construction operations, take sick people to the hospital, manage the edges of very big and very small public demonstrations, and do the best they could to keep themselves, their patients, residents, and inmates as safe as possible. Tragically, some of these people got sick, and a few of them died. Yet their colleagues and coworkers kept coming to work.

No one wrote much about this. I tried to talk about it. There have been many heroes throughout the pandemic. Let's never forget those public employees who showed up for every shift, every day, made constant adjustments on the fly as data and context and facts changed, and did it all while a lot of other people could simply hunker down in safety.

Sharing Purpose across Party Lines

As we write in the late fall of 2021, the Covid pandemic proves to be a continual test of the public trust at all levels of government. Covid taught us that even though government is pretty good at one-off natural disasters (winter storms, floods) and manmade disasters (transportation accidents, power outages, building fires), it was unprepared to address something of this magnitude and duration. We had had warnings of potential calamitous threats and emergencies, but our agencies had limited plans in place. Covid also highlighted gaps in the public sector's technology systems, logistics, and other critical operations that were necessary to address a sustained crisis at this scale.

Why were our public-sector operations so underprepared? That question will be debated by people who are a lot smarter than me and who will, I hope, offer up ways to improve our readiness and our response. But mulling that question takes me to a different issue: the way that partisanship dominates our national politics and big pieces of our state and local politics as well. Doing big things, especially big things that produce little political benefit, has become increasingly rare. I am old enough to remember when Republican President Ronald Reagan and Democrat House Speaker Tip O'Neill agreed on a fix to Social Security that dramatically improved the program's long-term financial outlook. It involved a combination of benefit and contribution policy changes that either side could have used to bludgeon the other in the upcoming elections. But by putting their personal political capital on the line, the two men took the cudgel away from the partisans. No one said a darn thing. And it worked.

These days, such a political investment by both parties at the national level is exceedingly rare. That means longer-term investments are very hard to make. The short term shared purpose around Operation Warp Speed, which produced effective vaccines to battle Covid in an incredibly short time, is a wonderful example of government leaders crossing party lines to make a seismic strategic difference in a time of emergency.

Similarly, the federal funding available to state and local governments through the American Rescue Plan Act of 2021 created an opportunity to make transformational, once-in-a-lifetime changes in housing, community building, education, environmental policy, and equity. But for now, it is only an opportunity. The product of all this possibility will be determined by *what* leaders choose to do with that funding, *why* they choose what they choose, and, perhaps most important, *how* they actually get it done.

Doing the right things with those resources, and doing them well, would go a long way toward building faith in government with our constituents—by showing them that we can do big things and do them well. And although a certain amount of partisanship exists in every decision made in the public square, I hope that leaders, given the enormity of the opportunity here, will take a page from the Reagan–O'Neill playbook and simply do what will make the biggest positive difference for the people and communities they collectively represent.

Stay Curious, Not Judgmental

At the start of this chapter, I quoted Philippians 2:3, the passage I shared with the congregation at the inaugural interfaith service: "Do nothing out of selfish ambition or vain conceit. Rather, in humility value others above yourselves." I've said before that I grew up with a mom who was a Democrat and a dad who, at ninety-three and counting, is a Republican. They were happily married for more than sixty years, took care of each other when they needed to, and showed their friends and their children what it meant to be completely and totally committed to someone else. They also almost never voted for the same person, and the debates around our dinner table were legendary among my friends. But they didn't debate character or motive. They debated *means*—how to best help someone.

The lesson I learned from watching them go at it was a simple one: the public square has plenty of opinions about how to help people and solve problems. Hear them all. Insight and knowledge come from curiosity and humility. Snap judgments—about people or ideas—are fueled by arrogance and conceit. They create blind spots and missed opportunities. Some ideas are more achievable than others, some cannot be acted on at all, and some can be executed only with the help of spectacularly talented people, a lot of money, and a ton of time. Too often, the *how* gets lost. Around our dinner table, that was always part of the discussion: "How are you going to do that?" The rhetoric came with a big scoop of confidence, but the *how* always came with two scoops of humility.

This book is about making sure that the *how* does not get lost. Be curious about how to make something happen, how to improve it, or how to make it last. Don't judge that as beneath you, or too dull to matter. In many cases, the *how* will define the success or the failure of your big idea. Building trust with the public is about commitment and follow-through. People don't expect you to get it right every time, but they do expect you to learn from your mistakes, appreciate what's possible, and execute.

· · ·

Finally, good ideas and interesting ways to accomplish goals in public life exist all over the place if you have the will, the curiosity, and the humility to find them—to listen. In the 1990s, we reorganized the way Health and Human Services purchased food and made meals at its twenty-four-hour facilities largely because of a visit I had with two women who climbed through many layers of bureaucracy to help me see that much of what we were doing wasn't working. We made a series of important changes in business processes and member services at Harvard Pilgrim as a result of listening to and cataloging what our members were saying.

If you are eager to make a positive difference in this grand endeavor we call public service, the Results Framework offers a way forward.

It doesn't always work, but it provides an organized way to tackle complex problems, take into account the unique circumstances of government, and adjust to failure without losing sight of the path ahead. It helped us get important work done—better and faster.

We hope that you will engage in meeting the challenges of public service. If you do, we hope this framework will help you succeed on behalf of your neighbors, your families, your friends, and your communities across the nation.

NOTES

Preface

1. David Brooks, "What Moderates Believe," *New York Times*, August 22, 2017, https://www.nytimes.com/2017/08/22/opinion/trump-moderates -bipartisanship-truth.html?searchResultPosition=1.

Introduction

1. Michael Wines and Amy Harmon, "What Happens When a Superspreader Event Keeps Spreading," *New York Times*, December 11, 2020, https://www .nytimes.com/2020/12/11/us/biogen-conference-covid-spread.html.
2. Michael Jonas, "Governor's Fix-it Man Exits," *CommonWealth*, Winter 2017, http://commonwealthmagazine.org/politics/governor-fix-its-fix-it-man/.

Chapter 1

1. Vijay Govindarajan and Christopher Trimble, *The Other Side of Innovation* (Boston: Harvard Business Press, 2010).
2. Vincent Canby, "The Tragedies of Bedlam in 'Titicut Follies' of 1967," *New York Times*, March 5, 1992, https://www.nytimes.com/1992/03/05/movies /the-tragedies-of-bedlam-in-titicut-follies-of-1967.html?searchResultPosition=1.
3. Yvonne Abraham, "At Last, Decency at Bridgewater," *Boston Globe*, September 13, 2017, https://www.bostonglobe.com/metro/2017/09/13 /turnaround/8XDF9RdNVvLGqpkjv8M4RK/story.html?p1=BGSearch _Overlay_Results.

Chapter 2

1. Mary Serreze, "Officials Celebrate Comcast Expansion in 9 Rural Western MA Towns," *Springfield Republican*, September 7, 2018, https://www .masslive.com/news/2018/09/state_celebrates_comcast_cable.html.
2. "Rowe Leaps Across the Digital Divide," Whip City Fiber, August 31, 2021, http://com-sprypoint-wge-whipcityfiber-static-site.s3-website-us-east-1 .amazonaws.com/2019/08/31/rowe-leaps-across-the-digital-divide/.

3. Larry Parnass, "Last of 'Last Mile' Towns Now Have Broadband Suitors," *Berkshire Eagle*, January 22, 2018.

4. Jed Pressgrove, "Massachusetts Pursues Its Own Route to Broadband Expansion," *Government Technology*, January 16, 2020, https://www.govtech .com/network/massachusetts-pursues-its-own-route-to-broadband-expansion .html.

Chapter 4

1. Nestor Ramos and Nicole Dungca, "With Riders at Wit's End, Beverly Scott Quits as MBTA Leader," *Boston Globe*, February 12, 2015, https://www.boston globe.com/metro/2015/02/11/mbta-general-manager-scott-given-vote-confidence -state-transportation-board/mqyFwO3DdME8NqkRU72ZlI/story.html.

2. Emma Platoff, "Pivots and Reversals Mark Governor Baker's Vaccine Rollout," *Boston Globe*, March 17, 2021, https://www.bostonglobe.com/2021/03 /17/metro/pivots-reversals-mark-bakers-vaccine-rollout/.

Chapter 5

1. Steve LeBlanc, "Gov. Baker Forces Resignation of 4 Health Connector Board Members," wbur.org, February 26, 2015, https://www.wbur.org/news /2015/02/25/health-connector-resignations.

2. Jess Bidgood, "Massachusetts Appoints Official and Hires Firm to Fix Exchange Problems," *New York Times*, February 7, 2014, https://www.nytimes .com/news/affordable-care-act/2014/02/07/massachusetts-appoints-official-and -hires-firm-to-fix-exchange-problems/.

3. Sarah Kliff, "How Massachusetts Screwed Up Obamacare," sarahkliff .com, June 6, 2014, http://www.sarahkliff.com/vox-work/2014/6/6/how -massachusetts-screwed-up-obamacare.

4. Priyanka Dayal McCluskey, "Sign-ups Surge on Mass. Health Connec- tor," *Boston Globe*, March 13, 2019, https://www.bostonglobe.com/business /2019/03/12/sign-ups-surge-mass-health-connector/O5UJZA6rvzqpw5k3ZL 2z9M/story.html.

Chapter 7

1. Bob Salzberg and Steve LeBlanc, "Report on Jeremiah Oliver Case: DCF Needs Overhaul, More Resources," *Sentinel & Enterprise*, May 29, 2014, https://www.sentinelandenterprise.com/2014/05/29/report-on-jeremiah-oliver -case-dcf-needs-overhaul-more-resources/.

2. The first recommendation was that DCF should revise its policies, practice guidelines, website, and written materials for consumers to consistently communicate that the agency's primary responsibility is to protect children and to make decisions in their best interests . . . and not according to a prescriptive hierarchy. See "Quality Improvement Report," completed by the Child Welfare League of America and submitted to Governor Deval Patrick and Secretary John Polanowicz on May 22, 2014; and Michael Levenson, "DCF Failures Didn't Lead to Jeremiah Oliver's Death Report Finds," *Boston Globe*, May 28, 2014, https://www3.bostonglobe.com/metro/2014/05/28/child-welfare-league -study-department-children-and-families-released-today/AviUhESS00YT wprWzSAPiK/story.html?comments=all&sort=OLDEST_CREATE_DT&p1 =Article_Inline_Text_Link&arc404=true.

3. Shira Schoenberg, "DCF Head Admits Agency Failed David Almond," *CommonWealth*, March 31, 2021, https://commonwealthmagazine.org/criminal -justice/dcf-head-admits-agency-failed-david-almond/.

4. Matt Stout, "As DCF Answers for Fall River Teen's Death, Advocates See 'Nightmarish Cycle' Replaying," *Boston Globe*, May 3, 2021, https://www .bostonglobe.com/2021/05/03/metro/dcf-answers-fall-river-teens-death -advocates-see-nightmarish-cycle-replaying/.

5. Stout, "As DCF Answers for Fall River Teen's Death, Advocates See 'Nightmarish Cycle' Replaying."

Chapter 8

1. According to "See How Vaccinations Are Going in Your County and State," *New York Times*, https://www.nytimes.com/interactive/2020/us /covid-19-vaccine-doses.html. This tracker uses CDC and Census Bureau data.

Epilogue

1. Lisa Wangness, "Charlie Baker's Service Signals Heft of Hispanic Church," *Boston Globe*, January 8, 2015, https://www.bostonglobe.com/metro /2015/01/08/growing-hispanic-church-hosts-inaugural-prayer-service /m5GcCbW0gJjMeK6gKLu0jJ/story.html.

2. Amy E. Lerman, *Good Enough for Government Work* (Chicago: University of Chicago Press, 2019).

3. William G. Howell and Terry M. Moe, *Presidents, Populism, and the Crisis of Democracy* (Chicago: University of Chicago Press, 2020).

INDEX

ACKNOWLEDGMENTS

While we are old gray-haired guys with lots of miles, we were just new kids when it came to writing a book. We didn't know the commonly understood rules of writing, understand the basic elements of how a book comes together, and that we must never, ever use mixed metaphors (old habits die hard).

We knew lots about how to get things done, but we had lots to learn about how to explain it. We needed, accepted, and sought out all kinds of help.

First, to Charlie's wife, Lauren, and to Steve's wife, Linda. The beginning, the middle, and the end of this book project, like so many of the most important things we have done, is about the support of our families and, most especially, Lauren and Linda. Honest truthtellers, deeply caring, seeing around the corners we don't, we are blessed, grateful, and can't believe how lucky we each are.

Second, to our colleagues over the years. You're the inspiration for this book. We thank you for the shared, lived experiences, and for the lessons learned about not only tactics and strategy, but also character. Grit, hope, persistence, creativity, and kindness in bucket loads each day.

Third, thank you to the individuals (Bruce B., Bruce V., Jane, Jeff, Julie, Kate, Katie, Mitch, Tam, Tom, and others, especially Mike K.) who took the time to read and provide their comments on our work in progress. Each point you made and question you raised pushed us to clarify what we were trying to say and how to express it. And special thanks to the Taubman Center for State and Local Government at Harvard Kennedy School for providing Steve a home base to do this writing.

Finally, to our editors Melinda Merino and Constance Hale. They pushed, prodded, and nudged to make an outline of concepts into something worth reading. Caterpillar to butterfly? Or maybe a moth? In any case, when we started we were just learning to walk and you helped us fly.

ABOUT THE AUTHORS

Charlie Baker is governor of Massachusetts. He has served as CEO of Harvard Pilgrim Health Care, a top-performing health-care insurance provider, and twice as Commonwealth of Massachusetts cabinet secretary leading the Executive Office of Health and Human Services and the Executive Office of Administration and Finance.

Steve Kadish has been CFO and COO, and held other senior leadership roles, in health care and higher education in both the public and the private sectors. He served as Governor Baker's first chief of staff. Steve is a senior research fellow at Harvard's Kennedy School of Government.

Charlie, a Republican, and Steve, a Democrat, have worked together tackling complex problems and developing result-oriented approaches over the three decades since they met in 1990.